AMERICAN ELF

THE COLLECTED SKETCHBOOK DIARIES OF JAMES KOCHALKA

BOOK TWO

JANUARY 1, 2004 TO DECEMBER 31, 2005

ISBN 978-1-891830-85-3

1. Graphic Novels
2. Autobiography
3. Cartoons/Cartoon Art

American Elf (Book Two): The Collected Sketchbook Diaries of James Kochalka
© 2007 by James Kochalka

Published by Top Shelf Productions, PO Box 1282, Marietta, GA 30061-1282, USA.
Publishers: Brett Warnock and Chris Staros.
Production: Christopher Ross. Publicity: Jacquelene Cohen.

Visit our online catalog at www.topshelfcomix.com
Read new diary strips each day at www.americanelf.com

First Printing, February 2007
Printed in China

AMERICAN ELF

THE COLLECTED SKETCHBOOK DIARIES OF JAMES KOCHALKA

BOOK TWO

JANUARY 1, 2004 TO DECEMBER 31, 2005

TOP SHELF PRODUCTIONS, MARIETTA, GEORGIA

INTRODUCTION

Hello Readers!

This book contains two full years of my daily diary comic strips.*

Lots of stuff happens

And... um... "end of introduction"

* AS ORIGINALLY SERIALIZED AT AMERICANELF.COM

JUNKIES

I found a hypodermic syringe in our trash outside

So, you know what that means...

...we've got JUNKIES

And do you have ants too?

Why? Are junkies afraid of ants?

JANUARY 1, 2004

AN ARBITRARY FEELING

Amy?

I was thinking

In my opinion, the first day of the new year is January SECOND, not January FIRST.

JANUARY 2, 2003

MY HIP HAS HURT FOR MANY YEARS. I THINK I HURT IT PERFORMING WITH MY BAND AND THEN DAMAGED IT FURTHER WORKING AS A WAITER.

IT GOT A LITTLE BETTER WHEN I QUIT THE PEKING DUCK HOUSE, BUT NOW IT'S GETTING WORSE AGAIN. SOMETIMES I GASP IN PAIN. IT'S EMBARRASSING.

GASP

JANUARY 3, 2004

SLOBBERY

help!

I got slobbered on

It's the slobber bandit!

That's highway slobbery!

JANUARY 4, 2003 *

*Misdated in original sketchbook

JANUARY 5, 2004

 A TASK FOR MY INTERN

SHE FOLDED AND STAPLED FOR ME,

THEN I HAD HER DO SOME SPRAY PAINTING.

JANUARY 6, 2004

MICROWAVING ELI'S BOTTLE, OR "PAVLOV'S BABY"

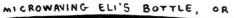

DECEMBER 7, 2003 *

JANUARY 8, 2004

HAVE YOU SEEN MY INTERN?

Let me introduce you to my intern.

Where is she? Where's my intern?

My intern my intern my intern ...

I just LOVE saying "My intern"!

JANUARY 9, 2003*

COLD IMPLOSION

IT'S A DRAFTY OLD HOUSE

AND THE COLD IS WICKED.

WE'RE SNUGGLED TIGHT UNDER THE COVERS...

... EXCEPT FOR ONE COLD EAR OF MINE THAT'S STICKING OUT.

JANUARY 10, 2004

DOUBTFUL SCRITCHING

SSSCRITCH

I'VE BEEN DRAWING THIS STRIP FOR OVER FIVE YEARS NOW

SSSCRATCH

DIGGING FOR A DEEPER MEANING

SSSCRIT S

BUT MOSTLY JUST SCRITCHING.

SCRITCH

JANUARY 11, 2004

ODDLY HAPPY

Mmm... so warm & cuddly

It's your fever.

Ooh?

Poor sick little bunny

Hawyaa

Are you hallucinating?

Mweh!

JANUARY 12, 2004

*Misdated in original sketchbook

COLD WAVE

I'm going to burn the drier lint.

Are you sure?
of course I'm sure

I mean, are you sure it's a good idea

It's the best idea I ever had!

JANUARY 13, 2004

FEELING THE FACE

SKULL SPLIT BY FROZEN AXE

EYES CRYSTALIZE

STEAM FROM BREATH FROSTING EYES

JAGGED ICE CAVE

NEEDLES OF ICE

CHEEKS STRETCHED AND SWOLLEN

SPLINTERING TEETH

CHEEKS BRITTLE AND CRACKING

SEARING PAIN AT BASE OF SKULL

JAN. 14 2004

THE SET-UP

HAGLARF

Eli's cough sounds like it's bubbling up through a bowl of pudding
It does?

Yeah! Well... what do you think it sounds like?
A little monkey cough
WARLF

Hey! Are you just trying to set me up to say something for your strip?

JANUARY 15, 2004

AN ARGUMENT BEGINS

What do you want to eat?

Well, what CAN we have?
Anything you want

Anything?
Then I'll take Thanksgiving dinner

Sigh
What?

JANUARY 16, 2004

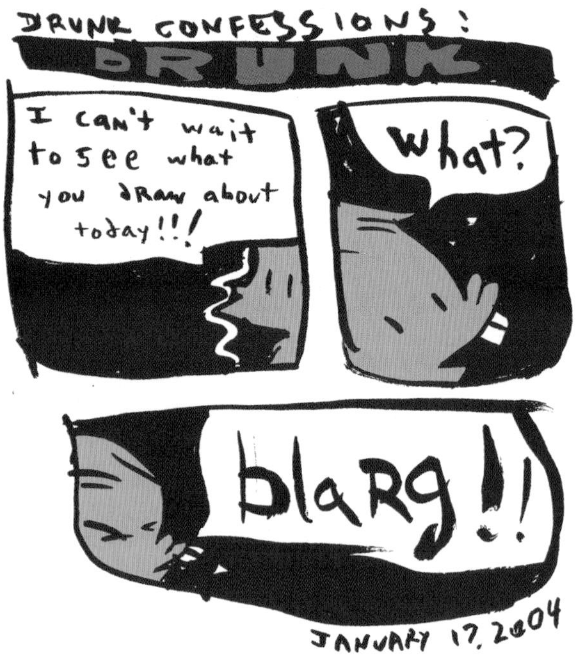
DRUNK CONFESSIONS:
DRUNK
I can't wait to see what you draw about today!!!
what?
blarg!!
JANUARY 17, 2004

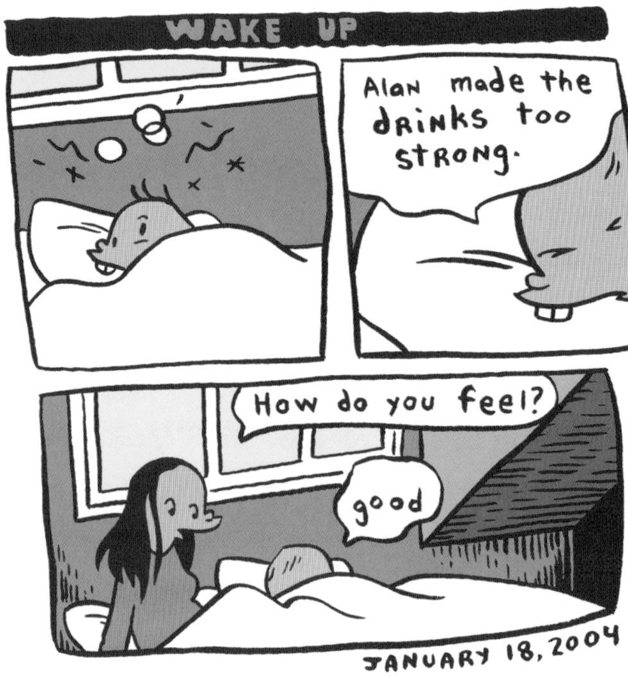
WAKE UP
Alan made the drinks too strong.
How do you feel?
good
JANUARY 18, 2004

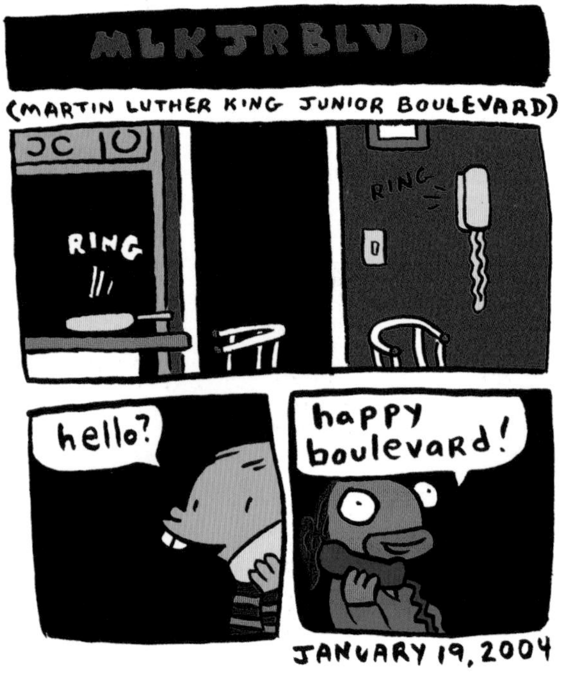
MLKJRBLVD
(MARTIN LUTHER KING JUNIOR BOULEVARD)
RING
RING
hello?
happy boulevard!
JANUARY 19, 2004

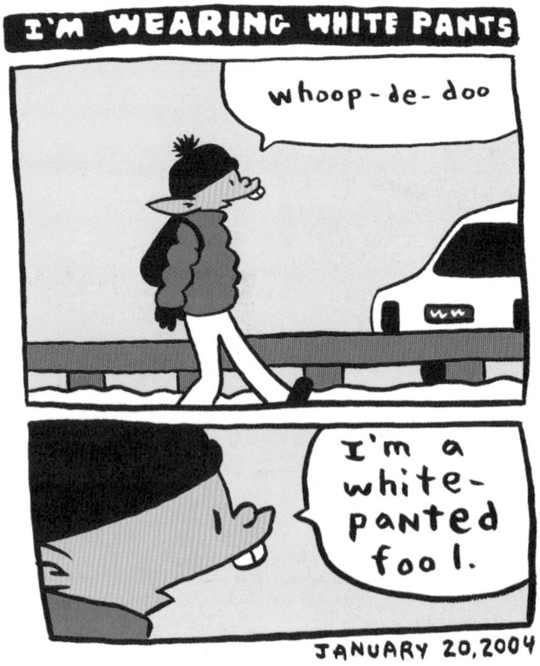
I'M WEARING WHITE PANTS
whoop-de-doo
I'm a white-panted fool.
JANUARY 20, 2004

JANUARY 21, 2004

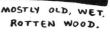

JANUARY 22, 2004

JANUARY 23, 2004

JANUARY 24, 2004

AUTOMATIC

Eli takes automatic doors for granted.

ALL doors are automatic to him!

JANUARY 25, 2004

WHILE WALKING BACK FROM DOWNTOWN, THE FLESH OF MY FACE SEEMED TO BE TRYING TO RETREAT FROM THE COLD. IT SEEMED TO BUCKLE AND TWIST AS IT TRIED TO WRIGGLE AWAY.

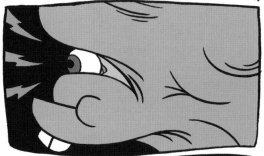

ALSO, TODAY I HAD FOUR PEANUTBUTTER COOKIES.

CRUNCH CHUNCH RUNCH

JANUARY 26, 2004

REVERSING POETRY

I'M TIRED OF BREATHING SOUR SMOKE

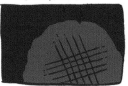

Burning rotten wood is not really working out quite as well as I said in my strip.

Well, maybe it was more poetic that way.

JANUARY 27, 2004

PANIC OF JOY

WITH THE WORDS "I'LL FEDEX THE CONTRACT TODAY"...

... I WENT INTO A PANIC.

help

JANUARY 28, 2004

EUCERIN® CREME

Grease up your cheeks

Grease up your leg

And your other leg

There! Now all your rashes are greased up!

JANUARY 29, 2004

AMY'S BIRTHDAY

I HUNG UP PAINTINGS...

I SWEPT & MOPPED THE FLOORS...

DID ALL THE DISHES & WASHED THE BATHTUB

& TRIED NOT TO THINK ABOUT THE RYKO CONTRACT FOR A WHILE.

JANUARY 30, 2004

BABY TALKING

pbpbpbbpp

HONK

GAAAAAAAAASP

PBPBPBPB

JANUARY 31, 2004

THE HUMAN EYE

THE WORLD LOOKS DIFFERENT THROUGH A DIGITAL CAMERA...

...IT'S A NEW PERSPECTIVE FOR A NEW AGE.

SET MENU DISP FUNC

NEW EYES & ANOTHER STEP TOWARDS OUR TRANSFORMATION INTO A RACE OF ROBOTS.

beep

FEBRUARY 1, 2004

RECORD DEALIO

ZING

I signed my soul for Rock and ROLL!

...IN QUINTUPLICATE! HA!

GROUNDHOG'S DAY!   FEBRUARY 2, 2004

GRUMPY COUNTRY

Do you want me to hold him?

Yes... but be careful. He's a little bit grumpy.

He's a little bit grumpy...

DADS ALWAYS MAKE LAME JOKES

but I'm a little bit Rock 'N' Roll

FEBRUARY 3, 2004

SPANDY CHECKS OUT THE NEW FURNACE:

FEBRUARY 4, 2004

LITTLE DANCE PARTY

MY INTERN HELPS ME GET MORE WORK DONE

If I put on some music, will you have a dance party with Eli while I work on some artwork?

SURE!

BUT I DON'T LIKE MISSING OUT ON ANY FUN.

FEBRUARY 5, 2004

BACHARACH GALLACTICA

RED WINE & BATTLESTAR GALLACTICA

Battlestar Burt Bacharach

Yeah, that's it.

FEBRUARY 6, 2004

NOZZLE COMICS

Awww

Look at this print out. I guess the nozzle needs cleaning

I don't know what's wrong. I just cleaned it.

Eli's nozzle needs cleaning too.

TWEAK

FEBRUARY 7, 2004

MY FRIEND JASON

Do you hate me?

What?

No!

Are you sure..? Maybe secretly, deep down inside?

No... well, you know...

You're JAMES.

I love you.

FEBRUARY 8, 2004

I SAT DOWN TO CONTEMPLATE MY EXISTENCE AND SEE IF I COULD DISCOVER SOMETHING NEW ABOUT MYSELF:

My elbow is cold.

FEBRUARY 9, 2004

CAN'T FIND IT

FUCK! Where is it!

LATER, AFTER AMY GETS HOME FROM WORK.

Here it is!

FEBRUARY 10, 2004

NANCY IS BROKEN

MY INTERN BROKE HER ARM.

ELI IS CONFUSED.

I can't pick you up

I'm so SORRY

I'M A LITTLE CONFUSED TOO.

FEBRUARY 11, 2004

THE EVIL ONES

A KITTY UNDER A TABLE AT JASON'S:

Don't bother. That cat is evil.

Oh, come on! You hate kitties, you hate baby talk... what DO you like?

I don't hate kitties!

Just the evil ones!

FEBRUARY 12, 2004

SILLY SWEET

CHOOSING CHOCOLATES FOR AMY...

... WHICH THEY PUT IN A BOX...

...and a "Dark Pistachio"

...AS I START TO TEAR UP...

... BECAUSE I'M SUDDENLY STRUCK BY HOW MUCH I LOVE HER.

FEBRUARY 13, 2004

A WARMTH ON THE BACK OF MY HEAD...

...AFTER MY ROCK SHOW...

...AFTER SOME BEERS...

... THERE'S A WARMTH ON THE BACK OF MY HEAD.

FEBRUARY 14, 2004

B A N G

Hey! You're PRETTIER THaN NoRmaL

How did you get PRETTiER?

I gave myself long bangs!

I thought it might make me look younger

Wow!

FEBRUARY 15, 2004

A LOT COOLER !?!

WHeN aRe you moving?! I don't **WANT** you to move to New YoRk!

Well... everyone should've been a lot cooler to me if they wanted me to stay...

I slow-danced with him on Valentine's Day, what more does he want?

FEBRUARY 16, 2004

W I N D O W

I think the Next dooR Neighbors might be dealing dRugs.

Amy Saw them hit Somebody with a pipe last Night.

Really?

OR maybe it was the Night before...

FEBRUARY 17, 2004

YESTERDAY'S EXCLAMATION

Da-da!

HOLY COW!

That's ME!

AND TODAY'S

Bla-bla!

Nooooo... Da-da!

I'm DA-DA

FEBRUARY 18, 2004

2/19/04

TODAY WAS HER LAST DAY AS MY INTERN... SO I DREW HER PORTRAIT AS A GOING AWAY PRESENT...

NANCY

—KOCHALKA

MY AMAZING LIFE

I WAS CLIPPING MY FINGERNAILS...

...WHEN ONE BOUNCED OFF MY EYEBALL.

CLIP

DOOINT

Amazing!

FEBRUARY 19, 2004

@#$@#@!?

What time are we planning on leaving tomorrow.

We didn't

Well, what time do you WANT to leave?

Not too late

Not too late, like "Late, but not too late", or not too late like "early"? What time do you WANT to go?!

I don't know

Not knowing when you want to go is the same thing as not wanting to go at all!!

Fine

FEBRUARY 20, 2004

I WAS THROWING UP ALL NIGHT, AND SICK ALL DAY WITH THE FLU. IT WAS AWFUL.

AWFUL SEXY

You're giving me a boner

I think it's 'cause my toe is touching you.

It must be one of your erogenous toes!

FEBRUARY 21, 2004

VISITING BABY'S GRANDPARENTS

ooh

Cough cough

Snif Snif

We're the sick family

Cough cough

Bringing disease to the elderly.

Snif Snif

FEBRUARY 22, 2004

MOM

MY MOM CORNERED ME AND TALKED ABOUT HER TAXES FOR TWO HOURS

Six hundred ninety three point seventy two

One thousand nine hundred and seventy five point fifty three

I don't care

thirteen dollars and eighty two cents!

why are you DOING THIS TO ME!?

FEBRUARY 23, 2004

MY FATHER'S DIARY

This is my diary entry from November 28

I don't know what year

"James opened his suitcase and said "It's frothing with clothes.""

Let me see

1986. I must've been coming home from college for a visit.

FEBRUARY 24, 2004

FFFIGHT!!!

I asked you to sit next to me on the couch and talk and you wouldn't even do it!

LATER

Wait a minute... yes I did!

FEBRUARY 25, 2004

ELI'S EYE INFECTION

Hey!

Eli stuck my nose in his eye. Now my nose is going to get Pink-eye!

That's the second time you said that today.

Well... it's contagious.

FEBRUARY 26, 2004

REASON FOR BEING

Look where the sky meets the mountain.

We had you so that you could experience the beauty of the world.

and because we wanted to meet you and see what you might be like.

FEBRUARY 27, 2004

TRIXIE'S MOUNTAIN
OR, TRY NOT TO BREAK YOUR DRAWING WRIST

Do you want to try a SNOWBOARD?

Naw, I'll just shred on a sled

DOOMF

You KNOW... I might as well try it.

Holy Cow!

unbelievable! impossible!

FEBRUARY 28, 2004

ELI CRIED ALMOST THE WHOLE WAY BACK FROM MAINE.

WE MADE UP ABOUT A HUNDRED NEW VERSES OF "THE WHEELS OF THE BUS GO ROUND AND ROUND"

The jewlrey on the bus goes bling-bling bling ♪

FEBRUARY 29, 2004

THE PERFECT BURP

uuuuuuRP

buurp. blaaRRRP URP!

bluuuuuRP! blep! Glarp

gluuuuuuuuRP

SEARCHING FOR A BURP THAT, ONCE BURPED, WILL MAKE ME FEEL BETTER.

MARCH 1, 2004

JASON BUYS ME LUNCH

OR, "DON'T MOVE TO NEW YORK"

You're preying on every fear and anxiety I have!

Well...

It's just because I don't want you to move away.

Well, you'll have to get used to it because I'm going.

What if you have another one of your attacks while you're driving down there?

MARCH 2, 2004

OH, THE TREASURES YOU'LL FIND

WHEN THE SNOW MELTS

WET TISSUE

BROKEN BEER BOTTLE

OLD DOG-SHIT

DEAD SQUIRREL

CIGARETTE PACK

LOTS MORE DOG SHIT

MARCH 3, 2004

BIG MISTAKE

Maybe it'd be fun to put another log in the fire

EEK!

Phew! I thought I had put my sketchbook in the fire!

MARCH 4, 2004

VORACIOUS

grr

RRRR

Did you learn how to read, Eli?

Oh, he's got a VORACIOUS appetite for Reading!

DUCK

MARCH 5, 2004

DREAMT REVIEW

I DREAMED A NEGATIVE REVIEW OF MY SKETCHBOOK DIARIES:

ONCE VITAL AND PASSIONATE, THE SKETCHBOOK DIARIES IS SLOWLY BUT SURELY DEGENERATING INTO A PALE SIMULACRUM OF ITS FORMER ESSENCE. THE STRIPS SEEM TO RELATE LESS TO REAL LIFE THAN THEY DO TO PREVIOUS STRIPS. THE DIARY IS BECOMING INCREASINGLY SELF-REFLEXIVE, DEVELOPING ITS OWN INTERNAL LOGIC. HOWEVER, IT IS A LOGIC INCREASINGLY DIVORCED FROM REALITY, AND INCREASINGLY INCONSEQUENTIAL.

MARCH 6, 2004

UNTITLED...

I think I might be too tipsy to draw.

OR... maybe I'm not tipsy ENOUGH.

STUPID

MARCH 7, 2004

WHEN IT SNOWS A LITTLE...

MY HEART MAKES A LITTLE LEAP OF JOY.

AND SO DO MY EYEBROWS.

MARCH 8, 2004

SKIZ-GLOTCH

MARCH 9, 2004

ANOTHER FEVER

MARCH 10, 2004

MY KITTIES

ELI HAS A DEEP COUGH.

HIS BREATH VIBRATES LIKE A PURR.

MARCH 11, 2004

SUPER SPIRALS

YESTERDAY, I NOTICED SOMETHING

Eli, your belly button is a SPIRAL!

THAT NIGHT I DREAMT ABOUT SPIRAL EYES.

ALSO, RIGHT BEFORE BED, I THREW UP.

MARCH 12, 2004

NTBO LG

Kelly & I have a BLOG. It's called "Half Dead and full of Hate."

Yeah!

Really? You? On the internet?

No. We keep our blog in a notebook.

That's not a BLOG...

That's a KLOG.

MARCH 13, 2004

DENTAL MIST

THE TOOTHBRUSH FLICKED OFF MY TEETH, SPRAYING A MIST OF TOOTHPASTE.

IT BURNED MY EYES A LITTLE.

MARCH 13, 2004

FLIGT OF THE WORM

I THOUGHT I SAW A WORM WIGGLE ACROSS THE SKY...

...BUT IT WAS A BIRD

MARCH 14, 2004

HEAVENGLAND

I donated a little painting to some cancer research charity in England.

Great. Well, you're going to heaven then.

I am?!

Well... in England at least.

MARCH 15, 2004

WHAT?

Huh? I didn't say much of anything.

IN HER PAJAMAS

Maybe I said "oh" or "uh" or something.

TIRED

THE END

MARCH 16, 2004

FINGER FRECKLE

WELL, LOOK AT THAT...

I HAVE A FRECKLE ON MY FINGER!

I WONDER IF IT WILL GO TO HEAVEN WHEN I DIE?

ANYHOW, I THINK IT'S SORT OF A SCAR FROM THE ECZEMA I USED TO HAVE.

MARCH 17, 2004

SOPHISTICATED DINNER PARTY

So, what made you decide to move to Burlington?

Well...

It seemed very sophisticated for its size.

I'M VERY sophisticated for MY size.

MARCH 18, 2004

HOME BASE

IT'S JASON'S LAST ROCK SHOW WITH ME BEFORE HE MOVES TO NYC, AND SO WE ROCK.

Guess how much money I made for my awesome ROCK show last night!

FOURTEEN DOLLARS!

Ha ha!

MARCH 19, 2004

SEPARATE

YESTERDAY, AMY STAYED HOME AND WATCHED ELI WHILE I WENT TO THE MOVIES TO SEE "ETERNAL SUNSHINE OF THE SPOTLESS MIND."

TODAY, SHE WENT TO SEE THE MOVIE WHILE I WATCHED ELI. I TOOK HIM DOWN TO THE BASEMENT AND WE PAINTED HIS HIGH CHAIR.

this is for you

WWAAAA

ON THE WAY HOME I BOUGHT HER SOME FLOWERS.

ON THE WAY HOME, AMY BOUGHT ME A PECAN TREAT.

Oh boy!! I'm going to eat it all in ONE BITE!

MARCH 20, 2004

ESCAPE

I REMEMBER YELLING...

Do you want to get wine or do you want beer?

WAAA

I DON'T KNOW

...AND JUMPING OUT OF THE CAR...

James!?! Be careful!

Fuck it

...BUT I DON'T KNOW WHAT THE FUCK I'M DOING...

HAPPENED LAST NIGHT, DRAWN MARCH 21, 2004

WAKE UP

NOW THAT I'M A DAD I HAVE TO DRINK COFFEE.

SIP

...BUT IT GIVES ME AN UPSET TUMMY.

UURRP

GURRRGLE

THAT'S ALL.

Maybe one more cup?

URRP!

MARCH 22, 2004

BABY TRUMPS KITTY

Trey Pieperdoodle from Crokeville, TN says "Don't hurt Spandy's feelings anymore".

Why did you hurt Spandy's feelings?

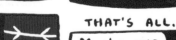

Oh... I told Eli that he was my favorite kitty...

I forgot about Spandy

It's hard to love a kitty when you have a baby.

MWA!

MARCH 23, 2004

BABY TRICKS

ELI FALLS ASLEEP WHEN YOU RUB HIS EAR:

WIGGLE WIGGLE

Z

HE ALSO CAN COUGH ON DEMAND:

Eli, cough cough!

Cough

He thinks it's his first word.

hee

MARCH 24, 2004

DRAWING WHILE WATCHING THURSDAY NIGHT TV

Nothing's coming out of my pencil.

MARCH 25, 2004

LINGERING INFAMY

WHEN I'M HOME ALONE IN THE MORNING...

I'M A LITTLE AFRAID TO TURN ON THE T.V.

I'M AFRAID THEY'LL SAY THE TWIN TOWERS GOT BLOWN UP AGAIN.

MY FRIEND JASON IS MOVING TO NYC NEXT WEEK.

I need a change.

MARCH 26, 2004

SPOONY E.

Eli loves Spoons.

Even if we take his spoon away from him at night, by morning he's somehow found another one!

That's why we call him "Spoony E."

MARCH 27, 2004

SONGWRITING

IS NOT AN EXACT SCIENCE...

Some people say that Jesus was a Robot..♪

No...

CREATION IS A FREE WHEELING PROCESS, A CONSTANT FLOW THROUGHOUT THE DAY, CHASING VARIOUS WHIMS. THIS IS TRUE FOR MUSIC, DRAWING, & WRITING.

MARCH 28, 2004

SPOONY SLAYS THE DRAGON

tAP tAP

You like your new spoon, don't you?

MARCH 29, 2004

HOLLYWUNK

$2281 to fly to Los Angeles. That's insane!!

Hmm... well... $568. That's a little better.

Still sucky

So... the ticket is $568, I guess. Should I do it?

Well... if someone buys our T.V. show idea, it's worth it. Otherwise, NO.

MARCH 30, 2004

Z

Oh, look.

The neighbor's dealing drugs.

MARCH 31, 2004

TWO VERMONTERS WATCHING TELEVISION

...two different offers*

Did they say "two Vermonters?"

NO

"Two different offers!"

Two Vermonters... that's US!

*"THE APPRENTICE"   APRIL 1, 2004

WOKE UP:
Do you know where the Missy Bly CD is?

blink blink

I want to listen to it on the drive to work.

uhh...

We've got the real album & we've got it on CDR also. Take the CDR so the real album doesn't get scratched up in the car.

O.K. Now get back to sleep.

No... I better stay up. If we're not equally tired when you get home from work, we'll fight.

APRIL 2, 2004

BREAKDOWN

It's hard to resist talking to you guys about videogames even though I know you're not interested.

So... you're going to anyway?

I'm resisting!

APRIL 3, 2004

OH BABY

Huh.

Maybe I'd rather not draw right now.

It'd be easier to just close my eyes and die...

waaaaa

APRIL 4, 2004

LUCKY LADY!

I almost bought you flowers today.

Almost! Thank you! Thank you!

I'm so Lucky!

APRIL 5, 2004

MUSICAL CEILING

That is the sweetest little sound...

FLAP FLAP FLAP

APRIL 6, 2004

IMPETIGO

Oh, that's a terrible sore, Eli

You don't seem to mind much, though.

LATER

Yeah... I guess he's doing okay ...except for the hole in his face.

What, you mean his mouth?

APRIL 7, 2004

COMPUTERY

SUCK SUCK SUCK

Honey...that's not a USB port!

That's your mouth!

POP

APRIL 8, 2004

SHE LIKES ME

WHILE RUNNING ERRANDS DOWNTOWN I STARTED TO FEEL NAUSEOUS SO I HEADED HOME TO THROW UP. WHILE CROSSING THE STREET THE CROSSING GUARD LADY STARTED TO SERENADE ME:

One of these days... la la la

What do you have in the manilla envelope?

Oh... um... just another envelope. ha ha!

You just made my day!

SMILE

APRIL 9, 2004

OUCH:

ELI'S ANTIBIOTICS AREN'T WORKING.

Poor sweet bunny... whimper

You only want to smile and play...

but your face hurts too much.

APRIL 10, 2004

HELP US

It seems like you, Eli, and Spandy are constantly CRYING for my attention.

We ARE!

whimper

WORSENING FACE INFECTION

RAGING DIARREAH

HAS A COUGH

meow!

NEEDS PETTING

APRIL 11, 2004

HUMOUR OF THE SICK

If mommy and daddy and Jesus can't cure him, I don't see how the doctors can.

Yesterday, while you were shopping and we were napping together, Jesus told me to drown the bunny in the bathtub.

That darn Jesus!

I KNOW!

He told me to drown myself in the tub, too.

I said how am I supposed to do that? And he said to use the futon to hold me down.

That wouldn't work

I KNOW

APRIL 12, 2004

REMEMBERED FROM AN EASTER DREAM.

SOBBING
ON THE CORNER OF THE BED

Waa... Eyah

Wah-ha-ha

Snif

Oh! I thought I heard you up here singing!

No.

ha ha

APRIL 13, 2004

BEST THING IN THE WORLD

His face looks like its getting a little better maybe.

See?

Right there?

It does!

Yes!

I FELT GOOD ALL DAY!

ha ha!

LATER

mm...food is the best thing in the WORLD

APRIL 14, 2004

TEMPORARY SOLUTION

A paint can lid.

It's just the Right size.

TO BLOCK OFF THE VENT THAT THE BIRDS ARE USING TO SNEAK INTO THE BATHROOM CEILING.

APRIL 15 2004

BICYCLE ENTHUSIASM

I think maybe the neighbors aren't really drug dealers after all.

Oh?

I guess I don't understand youth culture anymore. I think they might just be bicycle enthusiasts.

"youth culture killed my dog"

Unless...

Maybe their bicycle enthusiasm is just a cover...

APRIL 16, 2004

HOME TWEET HOME

AMY & TRIXIE MAKE ME UNCAP THE VENT SO THE BIRD FAMILY CAN MOVE BACK IN.

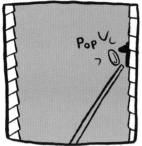

Pop U

Okay!

You can come back

APRIL 17, 2004

PREPARATION STAGE

I'm going to Kinko's to print out the "Millionaire Ape" stuff

Well, I hope you're a little bit NICER when you come back.

phoo

I don't think there's much chance of me being nice at ALL this week.

I'm so NERVOUS about my trip to L.A.

APRIL 18, 2004

THE BONERNET

Hey! You've got a boner.

Hi

Were you looking at naked GIRLS on the internet?

Just one

APRIL 19, 2004

HOW DO YOU DRAW "TOD SLEEPY"?

APRIL 20, 2004

ALL BETTER

YARD WORKIN'

APRIL 21, 2004

APRIL 22, 2004

POSSIBILITIES

APRIL 23, 2004

APRIL 24, 2004

AT RANDOLPH'S IN L.A. AND THE

MILLIONAIRE APE

clack clack clack

What would you say the "heart" of our show is?

Uh... what do YOU think the heart of our show is?

What do YOU think it is?!!

APRIL 25, 2004

EVERY SHOWER'S DIFFERENT

vvA vvA vvA

vvA vvA vvA

THE WAY THE WATER VIBRATED MY SKULL, IT SOUNDED LIKE THERE WAS A LITTLE HELICOPTER IN MY HEAD.

vvA vvA vvA

APRIL 26, 2004

PITCHES

That meeting went well.

I think so!

Should we high-five?

I think I sort of preferred yesterday's train wreck car crash of a meeting.

APRIL 27, 2004

SWEET AND SOUR SNOWGLOBE

James is like a snow globe from Vermont.

I am?

You shake it and inside is Amy, and Eli, and bands playing...

LATER

Today's meetings were horrible.

If no one buys the show then this was just a really stressful vacation that made me feel like an idiot.

APRIL 28, 2004

THE WORLD IS CRUEL

SLEPT ON THE AIRPORT FLOOR AT LAS VEGAS, USING MY SHOES AS A PILLOW.

WHICH PRETTY MUCH SUMS UP THE NINETEEN HOUR TRIP BACK HOME.

Snort

BUT MY BABY LOVES ME

Da Da!

I KNOW Eli, can you believe it?!!

It's Really ME

APRIL 29, 2004

L.A.MONADE

When life gives me lemons. I make lemonade.

CHOP

Literally!

Actually, Randolph gave them to me from his back-yard in L.A.

hey!

shake shake

SUGAR

We're almost out of sugar

APRIL 30, 2004

WEIRD LITTLE MICROPHONE

The medium of comics blah blah blah

Comics comics comics

Um...

COMICS SYMPOSIUM AT BENNINGTON COLLEGE

MAY 1, 2004

HOLY SHIT!

PARTYING WITH THE BENNINGTON STUDENTS WHILE AMY & ELI SLEEP.

LATER, I WAKE UP DISORIENTED, SHOCKED TO SEE THAT, APPARENTLY, I WENT HOME WITH SOME COLLEGE GIRL.

THEN, I NOTICE THE PORTABLE CRIB, THEN I NOTICE THAT THE GIRL IS MY WIFE, AMY.

MAY 2, 2004

POLICE CATS DON'T EAT PIE

SIRENS IN THE DISTANCE, MEOWING IN THE KITCHEN

MEEEEEEEEOOOOOW

Why won't she shut her pie hole?

She thinks that she's a little police car.

MEEEOC

MAY 3, 2004

MAY 4, 2004

RED

What's this?

I dunno. I guess I have hives.

Amy! They won't let me give blood because I have HIVES on my arms.

That's lucky for you! You got so nervous, you gave yourself hives. I hate giving blood.

MAY 5, 2004

THE LAST EVER EPISODE OF F R I E N D S

James!?!

I love those guys.

LATER

Is it lame to draw a strip about watching T.V.?

No way! It's AWESOME

MAY 6, 2004

WORK HARDER

God... I need a cup of coffee. I could go out and get some, but UPS is supposed to deliver my packages today. I gotta be here.

CLICK CLIC CLICK

If I still had my intern, I could send her out for it.

CLICK CLICK

Spandy is doing a sucky job as her replacement

CLICK !!!

LATER
Spandy! You threw up on the carpet again?!

You're the worst intern EVER

MAY 7, 2004

DWARFISM

Eli's making me sleepy & grumpy.

He's making ME dopey, happy, sneezey and bashful.

meh!

?!

What about Doc?

MAY 8, 2004

VIRTUAL FRIENDSHIP

JASON CALLS FROM NYC ON HIS CELL PHONE

Oh, Hi Jason!

How are you?

Do you know where "See Hear" is?

I can't find it

Hold on, I'll check on the internet. Let me switch to my cordless phone.

It's 59 E 7th St. Between 2nd and First.

Oh, I see it now.

Thanks

Gotta go

MAY 8, 2004

HER OWN DAY

PICKING FLOWERS WHILE AMY SLEEPS LATE

This will show mommy how much we love her.

MOTHER'S DAY

MAY 9, 2004

SUDDENLY DORITOS

TALKING TO CRESTON ON THE PHONE

Suddenly, I want some Doritos

I'm going to walk to "Dot's". Let's see how far this cordless phone will take us.

giggle giggle

What? You're breaking up. It's all static.

Wait, now it's better.

I think this tree is acting as an antenna!

Ha ha

MAY 10, 2004

I SHOWER SECOND

Amy, which towel is mine?

The light one or the dark one?

The DRY one!

They're both wet!

Well, then they're both MINE.

hey!

MAY 11, 2004

SPECIAL FRIEND

Huh! He's playing with a sun-beam

Goo

Just like a goddam "Hi & Lois" comic strip!*

MAY 12, 2004

* WHO WOULDA GUESSED THAT SHIT WAS REAL?

ELI FELL ASLEEP IN THE STROLLER ON THE WAY BACK FROM RUNNING OUR ERRANDS. WHEN WE ARRIVED HOME, I UNBUCKLED HIM AND THEN WENT TO UNLOCK THE DOOR. THAT'S WHEN I REALIZED THAT I HAD FORGOTTEN MY P.O. BOX KEY BACK AT THE POST OFFICE, SO I GRABBED ELI AND HURRIED BACK DOWNTOWN:

The wheel is stuck.

CRUNK

WAAA!

ELI, UNBUCKLED, HAD FALLEN FACE DOWN ONTO THE PAVEMENT AND I HAD RUN HIM OVER. HIS LITTLE ANKLE WAS TWISTED BETWEEN THE WHEELS.

MAY 13, 2004

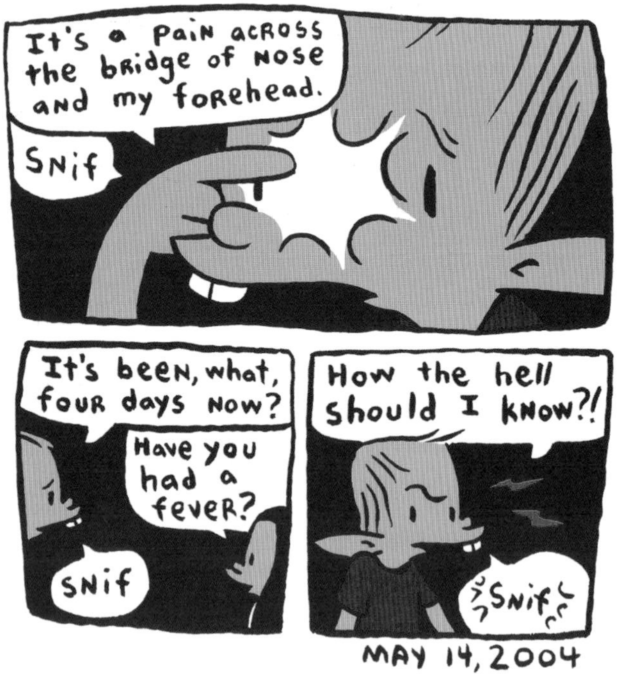
It's a pain across the bridge of nose and my forehead.
Snif
It's been, what, four days now?
Have you had a fever?
Snif
How the hell should I know?!
Snif
MAY 14, 2004

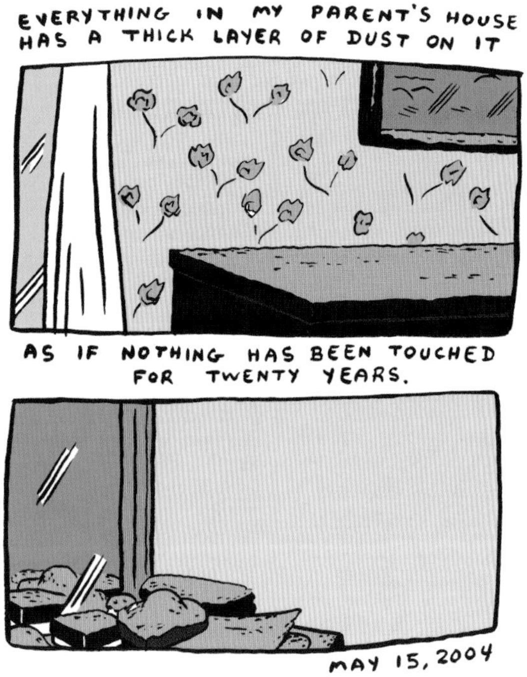
EVERYTHING IN MY PARENT'S HOUSE HAS A THICK LAYER OF DUST ON IT
AS IF NOTHING HAS BEEN TOUCHED FOR TWENTY YEARS.
MAY 15, 2004

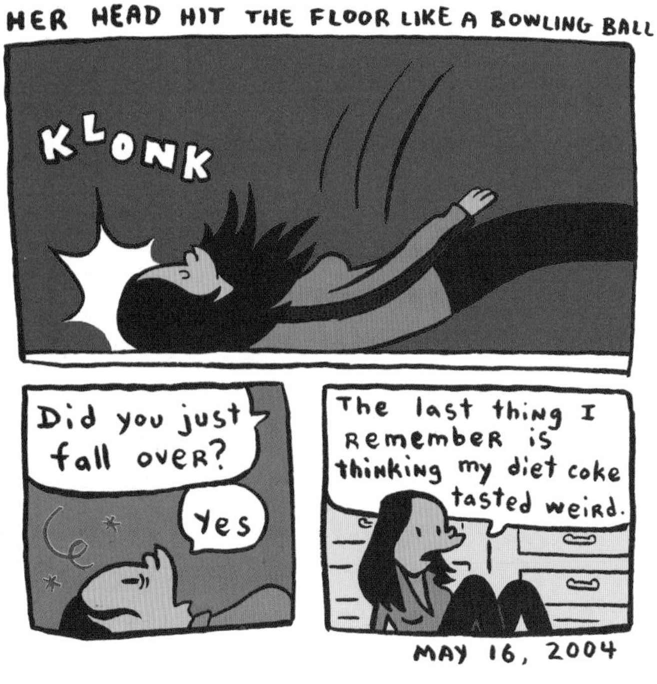
HER HEAD HIT THE FLOOR LIKE A BOWLING BALL
KLONK
Did you just fall over?
Yes
The last thing I remember is thinking my diet coke tasted weird.
MAY 16, 2004

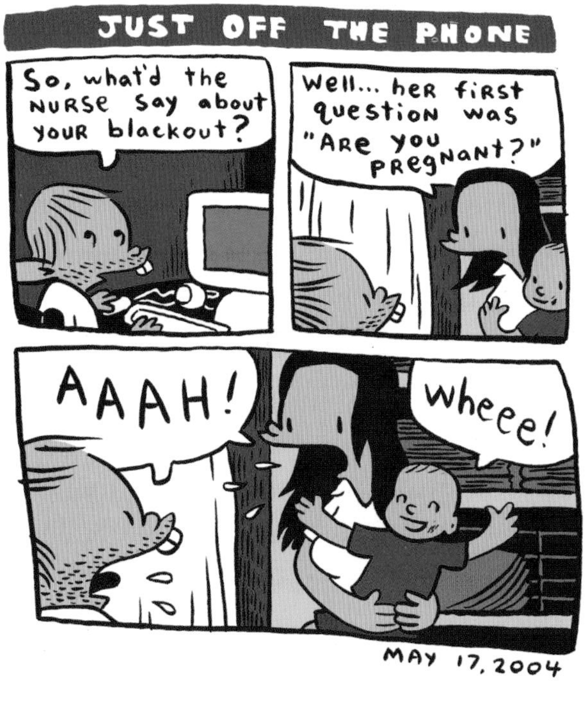
JUST OFF THE PHONE
So, what'd the nurse say about your blackout?
Well... her first question was "Are you pregnant?"
AAAH!
Wheee!
MAY 17, 2004

COSMIC VISION

Amy, look

I was growing a third eye ...but I picked it off

SMOKE ALARM TEST

sshhh

MAY 18, 2004

EYE BURN

Gah!

This sun screen is burning my eyes

eRmf

I can't believe I actually put it right on his eyelids!

Oh, bunny!

I'm sorry

MAY 19, 2004

THE BETRAYAL

How's Jason?

He betrayed me

By moving away?

Yes!

HAPPY NOTHING

Amy, let's cancel my birthday party.

Why?

I forgot to invite anyone, now it's too late

Where's the phone? I'll do it.

MAY 20, 2004

HOSE THE GRIME

HOSING THE WINTER GRIME OFF THE PORCH GETTING READY FOR MY BIRTHDAY PARTY

MAY 21, 2004

PARTY GUESTS

A GROUP PORTRAIT OF ALL WHO ATTENDED MY BIRTHDAY PARTY BRUNCH:

AMY · ELI · SPANDY · JOSH
KELLY · KERRIE · CRESTON · CHRIS B · COLIN
ERIC O · KATE · JEFF · LAUREN · ASA · LILLY
STEVE McQUEEN · JEN · JOHNY O · JONAS · JEFF MASON ON THE PHONE

MAY 22, 2004

SUPER INTIMACY

Yesterday, when we were having sex and I called out your name...

I almost accidentally called out "ELI" instead of "AMY"

ha ha

blehhh

MAY 23, 2004

ELI'S FIRST FART JOKE

PRRAP

≀giggle≀

RECOGNITION

When my big diary strip collection comes out in July, do you think anyone will offer me an honorary PHD?

No.

But I've worked so HARD!

MAY 24, 2004

WATCHING THE BABY

Z

WAK!

ELI!?

Da!

Phew

MAY 25, 2004

THE PRESENT

"Wake up, "Daddy"!"

"Happy birth-day"

"DA!"

"Eli has a COLD SORE"

"Weee!"

MAY 26, 2004

MFA

YESTERDAY, I DREAMT OF UNCOVERING A SUPPRESSED MEMORY,

AND I WOKE UP CONVINCED THAT I HAD MURDERED SOMEONE BACK IN GRADUATE SCHOOL.

"Shit!"

TALKING TO MY SISTER:

"No, no, I'm SURE I didn't kill ANYONE! I did have a roomate that jumped off a bridge and killed himself, though."

"Maybe you pushed him."

MAY 27, 2004

BEING KOCHALKA
A DRUNKEN CARTOONIST INTRODUCES HIMSELF

"Everybody wants to be James Kochalka"

"They all want to BE you"

"Noo"

"You're teasing"

MAY 28, 2004

BIKINI POWER
I GOT A BONER AS SOON AS SHE CHOSE IT OFF THE RACK

"Buy it! OR at least try it on"

"I don't know... my boobs droop ...my tummy"

"You can just wear it to bed with me then! Buy it!"

MAY 29, 2004

FLOATING ON THE LIGHT

I FOCUSED CAREFULLY ON THE SWIRLING FLOATING DUST.

FIRST THING IN THE MORNING, MAY 30, 2004

CHECK ONE

A FAMILY IS TEARING UP THE HILL BEHIND MY HOUSE WITH THEIR ALL-TERRAIN-VEHICLES. SHOULD I:

■ TELL THEM TO STOP?

■ IGNORE IT?

God, why do you even let that bother you? Why even think about it?

I'm becoming a cranky old man.

MAY 31, 2004

ELI SLEPT ALL DAY WHILE I HAD
BORING ADVENTURES

RahR

CRUNCH CRUNCH

RUSTLE

I ate all the potato chips today.

Why?

I was SO BORED

JUNE 1, 2004

GLOTCHIN'?

SILVER RATTLE.

JING JING JING JING

UNBELIEVABLY LOUD, STIFF CRINKLY PLASTIC.

CRASH CRASH

CRASH

CLAP CLAP

CLAPPING.

What'd you do today?

Shhh

me and Eli started a band. It might be the world's first genuine SKIZ-GLOTCH group!

JUNE 2, 2004

DUCK HAT

I DO ENJOY CARING FOR MY BABY BOY AND I REALLY WOULDN'T TRADE IT FOR ANYTHING, BUT IT'S ACTUALLY SORT OF TEDIOUS TO PLAY ALL DAY LONG!

Uh-oh, Eli

Ducky's wearing a hat again

LATER

Uh oh!

JUNE 3, 2004

MOMENTS OF THE DAY

How could I have drawn something so awful, so recently? I suck.

Why am I so much awesomer than other people?

I wish I could erase everything that's ever happened to me.

I really have a unique and special talent ... for something or other.

OUT OF ORDER, JUNE 4, 2004

PINK RIBBON

WHEN SPANDY WAS A KITTEN I USED TO PLAY WITH HER,

BUT AS SHE GOT OLDER I SORT OF FORGOT ABOUT THAT AND I HAVEN'T REALLY PLAYED MUCH WITH HER IN YEARS.

BUT THE OTHER DAY, THIS PINK RIBBON CAUGHT MY ATTENTION.

LET THE GAMES BEGIN!

JUNE 5, 2004

FAREWELL, MY OLD NEMESIS

Remembering Ronald Reagan

FUCK Reagan.

JUNE 6, 2004

RASH

ELI HAD AN EAR INFECTION, BUT THE ANTIBIOTICS (COMBINED WITH EXPOSURE TO THE SUN) CAUSED AN ITCHY RASH.

eRmf

NOW THERE'S A MEDECIN FOR THE RASH, WHICH MAKES HIM SLEEPY.

WE TRULY LIVE IN A WORLD AT WAR. VIOLENT CONFLICT RAGES ACROSS EVERY SQUARE INCH OF THIS EARTH. THE FUNDAMENTAL ENERGY OF THE UNIVERSE IS DISCORD AND STRIFE, AND IT IS THIS ENERGY FROM WHICH ALL LIFE ARISES. IT'S A WICKED, WICKED WORLD.

JUNE 7, 2004

I ALREADY ATE

Hey James, this is Jason. I'm on Church Street! Have you eaten yet?

Phh! You fuckin' dick.

Well...

Should I just come over to your house?

NICE VISIT,   JUNE 8, 2004

ACCURACY

By the way, when I called you yesterday it was from a pay phone. My cell doesn't work up here.

But you got the location right, in your strip. That's right where I was standing

What about your cell phone, though? I drew it as the flip-up silver kind.

No... it's blue with a little short antenna.

It's not the flip-up kind

JUNE 9, 2004

QUICK AND STORMY

YESTERDAY A STORM MOVED IN SUDDENLY

WOOSH...

WOOOSH

THE POWER WENT OUT WHILE I WAS TALKING TO JASON.

BOOM
Yikes

I FOUND MYSELF HALF WISHING THAT MY COMPUTER WAS FRIED, SO I COULD GET A NEW ONE.

JUNE 10, 2004

JAZZ FESTIVAL

Don't they know what that means?

They might as well call it the FUCK Festival

JUNE 11, 2004

TALL GRASS

WISSHHHH

WOOOOOSHHH

SHHHEEERR

JUNE 12, 2004

I HAVE A NEW FRIEND TO TALK ABOUT COMICS WITH, BUT MORE IMPORTANTLY, WE PLAY ...CROQUET!!!!!!

POP

YOUR TURN CHRIS

KLUK

POONT

BLONK

JUNE 13, 2004

"OFF THE HOOK"

OR, "THE WIND AND I"

This wind is like totally "in your face"!

IT'S EXHAUSTING!

JUNE 14, 2004

MEAN SPIRITED

A WEEK AGO, THE DENTAL HYGENIST POKED ME A BIT. SHE HURT ME. SINCE THEN I'VE BEEN FUSSING OVER THE WOUND, MAKING IT MUCH MUCH WORSE. I WENT BACK TO THE DENTIST TODAY.

Why am I such a jackass?

God is punishing you for being mean to me.

But I'm only MEAN to you because God is PUNISHING me!
Because I'm such a little angel?
and you knew that I could deliver the message?

JUNE 15, 2004

DIZZYING SHIMMER

A HOT GLARE SHIMMERS FROM THE POWER LINES

WHILE WHITE TREE FLUFF FLOATS BY...

AND JET FIGHTERS SCREAM THROUGH THE AIR.

BLAM

JULY 16, 2004 *

THE INITIAL ORDERS FOR THE "AMERICAN ELF" BOOK COLLECTION CAME IN ABYSSMALLY LOW,* BUT I WON'T LET THAT STOP ME!

HA HA HA

Okay, here we go!

Sigh

It's hard to draw good comics when you're depressed.

* ONLY 600 COPIES

JULY 17, 2004 *

BOOTY SHAKER

booty shaker booty shaker boom boom
shake
shake shake

Eli you're making me hoarse with all this singing. Can I take a break?

WAAAA

HE TAKES HIS MUSIC VERY SERIOUSLY...

LATER
Rattle Rattle
shake shake

JULY 18, 2004 *

*Misdated in original sketchbook

what do you expect from Father's Day, tomorrow?

Nothing

JULY 19, 2004 *

BUMP
BUMP THUMP

HAPPY FATHER'S DAY!

The Greatest Day of the YEAR!

MATCHING GREEN CAP & BOXERS: MY FATHER'S DAY PRESENTS!

JUNE 20, 2004

WORLD OF THE CARTOONIST

MORE THAN EVER, MY VISION IS TURNED INWARD, TOWARDS MY FAMILY.

WITH NO "JOB" TO DISTRACT ME FROM MY LITTLE UNIVERSE, I BARELY EVEN KNOW WHAT DAY OF THE WEEK IT IS. *

Yawn

Amy, my toe hurts

Did you stub it?

I have no recollection

JUNE 21, 2004

* I DIDN'T NOTICE THAT I HAD BEEN MISDATING THESE STRIPS LAST WEEK UNTIL SOMEONE TOLD ME.

JAY OH BEE

FIRST DAY OF AMY'S SUMMER VACATION

Is this how you're going to act all summer?!

Maybe you should get a JOB

What?! Noooooo

JUNE 22, 2004

AUNT MARGY

Hmm? Oh, well, I'm going on a book-signing tour in a few weeks.

The book's called "AMERICAN ELF". It's my diary.

No... I don't really want to send you one. No, I don't want you to buy it, either

It's PRIVATE!

It's my diary

JUNE 23, 2004

WEED PULLER

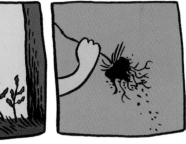

Yeow! I've torn the skin right off my finger

JUNE 24, 2004

I JUST NOTICED ALL OF A SUDDEN.

ALL GOD'S CREATURES

Eli's chasing an ant

I'll kill it

SLAP

WAAAA!

← DEAD

JUNE 25, 2004

THE COMIC STRIP I WAS BORN TO DRAW: SQUEAKY & LEAKY

I'm not sure I want the leftover potato salad. The skins are too squeaky when my teeth bite them

stop complaining

Hey... it tastes different than it did yesterday.

better OR worse?

WORSE! Now it's all watery.

I think the tomatoes are leaking.

JUNE 26, 2004

I PLAYED A BRILLIANT GAME OF CROQUET... BUT I STILL LOST.

LATER, A LITTLE DRUNK & VERY TIRED, I DREW A STRIP ALL ABOUT IT.

THEN, I ERASED IT AND WENT TO BED...

DRAWN THE MORNING AFTER JUNE 27, 2004

DOMINATE THE DAY

CLOUDS FORMED

AND TURNED DARK

BUT NEVER TURNED TO RAIN,

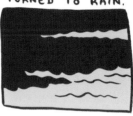

THE ANTICIPATION DOMINATED THE DAY.

JUNE 28, 2004

LATE LATE THOUGHTS

God... I love little Eli so bad.

If anything ever "happened" to him, I'd punch myself in the fucking face until I DIED.

JUNE 29, 2004

IT'S MY DIARY, NOT HIS

How's your son's impetigo?

Oh, it turns out it was NEVER impetigo

It's something else

Should I say "herpes"?

↓NEW HAIRCUT

I don't want the strip to become just a catalog of Eli's outbreaks & sicknesses.

OR YOUR OWN

I should BAN myself from drawing about them

Draw one about THAT!

oh, I will

JUNE 30, 2004

24 DOLLAR HAIRCUT

I GOT A NICE PROFESSIONAL HAIRCUT FOR OUR WEDDING ANNIVERSARY

BUT THIS MORNING, I CAN'T SHAKE THE FEELING THAT I'M A MURDERER...

BECAUSE I HAVEN'T DONE ENOUGH TO STOP GEORGE W. BUSH'S INSANE WAR.

MY SHIT IS BLOOD RED

...FROM THE BEETS I ATE.

JULY 1, 2004

SUMMER VACATION

BAM

Eli's messing with your clothes, Amy!

Well, we've got to fold them before we leave on our trip. He's just helping.

Damn, Amy! Your little shirts are SEXY!

JULY 2, 2004

I'M LIKING MAINE

I like the dead pine trees covered in lichen

I'm LIKIN' them!

JULY 3, 2004

FACEFULL OF SAND & FOG

BABY HIKING

ouch   my throat   my hip

SICK IN BED

I don't want to miss Eli's first fireworks

BORN IN THE USA

WEEOOOO   BOOM

JULY 4, 2004

LEAVING MAINE

There's sand in my shoes

I can feel it

hooRay!

FINALLY HOME

THE SAND IS MADE OF TINY FRACTIONS OF SEASHELLS.

I SPRINKLE IT FROM MY SHOE TO OUR BACK YARD.

JULY 5, 2004

TONSILLECTOMY

No, James. You can't have your tonsil removed!

why not?

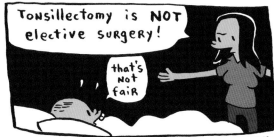

Tonsillectomy is NOT elective surgery!

that's not fair

JULY 6, 2004

BOOK STORE BOYS

and is that Eli?

Yeah. Be careful ... he's pretty CRANKY.

why, he doesn't LOOK cranky.

AAAAAA!

oh!

JULY 7, 2004

NOT VERY PUNK ROCK

This sunscreen is specially formulated for baby faces

That's good, I guess.

That's the kind of face he's got.

JULY 8, 2004

FAMILY FUN TIME

James, Eli wants you to smell his butt.

Oh?

What's it smell like?

Mint?

Flowers?

Candy?!

SNIF SNIF

Poo.

Arg!

Tricked again!

JULY 9, 2004

TOO CUTE

Paige says Eli is so cute that she can't stand lookin' at him.

JULY 10, 2004

CHOCOLATE PLANE CRASH

I think I'll have more chocolate.

You don't need more chocolate!

But what if I die in a plane crash this week?

(AT MY PARENT'S HOUSE) JULY 11, 2004

ELI LOST HIS NAT

AND WE'RE LOOKING FOR IT.

SCANNING...

UNABLE TO LOCATE TARGET

SCANNING

SECONDARY TARGET LOCATED

mmm

KISS

uh uu

TARGET ELIMINATED

JULY 12, 2004

A BRIEF REPRIEVE

Do you think I'll miss you guys so much I'll be crying and clawing at my chest the whole time I'm gone?

No... probably just an hour or two a day

LATER, LAYING ON THE COUCH, WAITING TO LEAVE:

RING

This flights been delayed by 100 minutes

Do you need a pen?

JULY 13, 2004

JIM HANLEY'S UNIVERSE

THE FIRST SIGNING OF THE TOUR. NYC.

What the FUCK!

It's Not here! How could the store Not be here?!

This is fucking IMPOSSIBLE! I've been walking up & down this block for an HOUR!

Oh... it's on 33rd. This is 34th.

Ha ha

JULY 14, 2004

PLEASE HELP ME

Rustle

When I go...

...could you help me hail a cab?

You've never done it before?

Not successfully

LEAVING NYC —

JULY 15, 2003

AT WAYNE'S HOUSE

THEN CHICAGO COMICS

Have you been having fun in Chicago?

Well... I read Entertainment Weekly for seven hours.

JULY 16, 2004

STUFF THAT HAPPENS WHILE I'M GONE

SPANDY RUNS AWAY:
Spandy? ay-yah?

SPANDY COMES BACK:
Meow

ELI GETS A CLOTHES HANGER CAUGHT IN HIS THROAT:
Help! Somebody HELP! WAAA

JULY 17, 2004

READING FRENZY

What day is it? Where am I?

This tour is making me feel weird.

THE OTHER SIGNINGS HAVE BEEN VERY SUCCESSFUL FOR BOTH ME & CRAIG... BUT HERE IN HIS HOME TOWN I MIGHT AS WELL NOT EVEN EXIST.

Fuck

PORTLAND, OR

JULY 18, 2004

OXBOW

First, you gotta acclimate the scrotum...

No, you've got to dive right in. It's total body shock but at least your balls don't notice.

JULY 19, 2004

SAMAURI COMICS PRESENTS:

WHAM!

Wow!

The sun is INCREDIBLE

Holy cow!

LATER My eyes burn.

PHOENIX, AZ

JULY 20, 2004

IN THE BAR WHERE THEY FILMED "TOP GUN"

God!! I'd kill myself before I'd get a divorce!

Before?!

!

hee hee hee hee hee hee

Yeah...

SAN DIEGO, CA

JULY 21, 2004

NERVOUS COFFEE WIGGLES

Maybe more coffee will help me shit easier

SIP

You've got to try to shit a little every DAY ♪

SIGNING BOOKS:

Woah

See that line I drew? ... ...that's the coffee wiggles!

JULY 22, 2004

ROOM SERVICE

I'll shake Jim's hand goodbye and kiss Peggy on the cheek

Thanks for the sandwhich

FAMOUS SUPERHERO ARTIST

goodnight Peggy

JULY 23, 2004

BITCHING ABOUT COMICS

bitch bitch bitch

bitch bitch

bitch bitch

ha ha

bitch!

JULY 24, 2004

EISNER AWARD

SLURP

I sort of stole this glass by accident

I'm going to bring it home and tell Amy that I won an Eisner award and this is it

JULY 25, 2004

EMPTY ACHE IN THE AIRPORT

I NEED TO RETURN HOME.

EARLY IN THE BOOKSIGNING TOUR I FLIPPED A LITTLE SWITCH OFF, INSIDE ME.
CLICK

I DID THIS SO THAT I MIGHT NOT MISS AMY & ELI QUITE SO BADLY.

I **NEED** TO RETURN HOME.

JULY 26, 2004
CHICAGO O'HARE

RETURN OF THE ELF

OH, IT'S GOOD TO BE BACK HOME.
Ow! My Nipple
PINCH

AMY SAID A MILLION FUNNY THINGS TODAY:
hee hee ha ha hoo

I THINK I GOT FATTER ON THE TOUR
Amy?
what do you think?

JULY 27, 2004

CHEAP HOTEL

Huck

I don't know what I just saw down the drain but it made me almost puke

I think it's a cigarette butt.
God, I thought it was a severed finger

MONTREAL

JULY 28, 2004

SHREK 2

Here Eli, play with "Shrek 2"

meow?

He meows at all his toys now

JULY 29, 2004

MICROWAVE WINE

"Microwave the wine"?!

What?! I didn't say that!

I think I just said "Do you want me to POUR the wine?"

Oh!

Besides, it's too HOT to drink microwaved wine today

JULY 30, 2004

TINY BUBBLES

Watcha doing?

looking at my finger

Why don't you write a graphic novel about it?

I did

It didn't help much

JULY 31, 2004

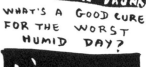

NO BIG REVELATION, DRAWN DRUNK

WHAT'S A GOOD CURE FOR THE WORST HUMID DAY?

A FEW BOTTLES OF WHITE WINE WITH YOUR FRIENDS:

BEREFT OF MEANING, YET FULL OF LIFE.
-AUGUST 1, 2004

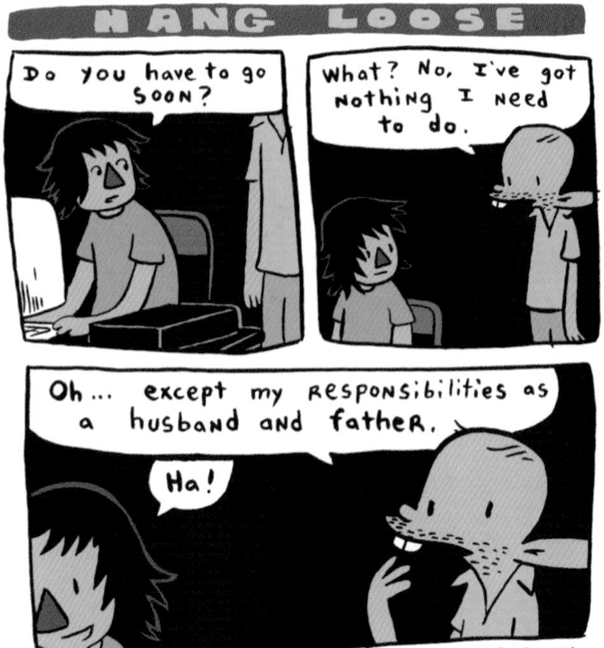
HANG LOOSE
Do you have to go soon?
What? No, I've got nothing I need to do.
Oh... except my responsibilities as a husband and father.
Ha!
AUGUST 2, 2004

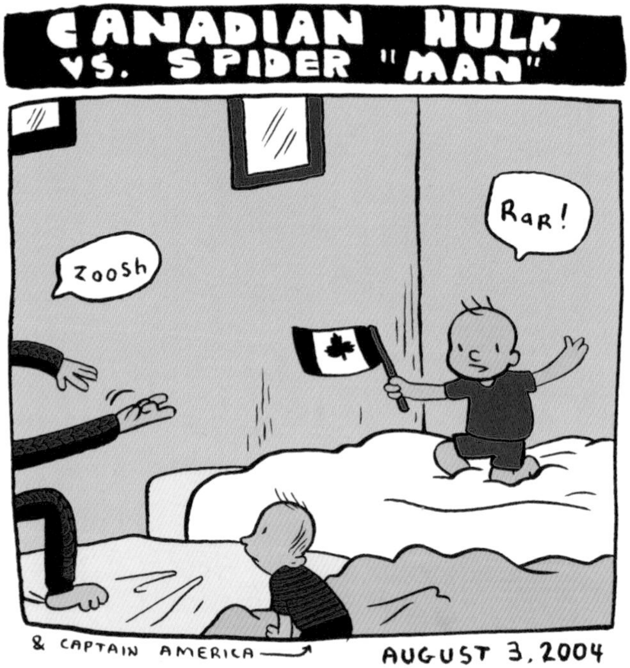
CANADIAN HULK VS. SPIDER "MAN"
Zoosh
Rar!
& CAPTAIN AMERICA
AUGUST 3, 2004

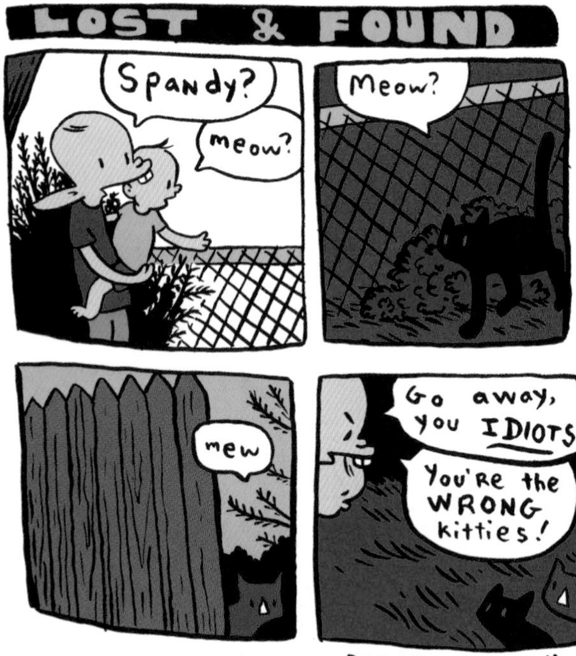
LOST & FOUND
Spandy?
meow?
Meow?
mew
Go away, you IDIOTS
You're the WRONG kitties!
AUGUST 4, 2004

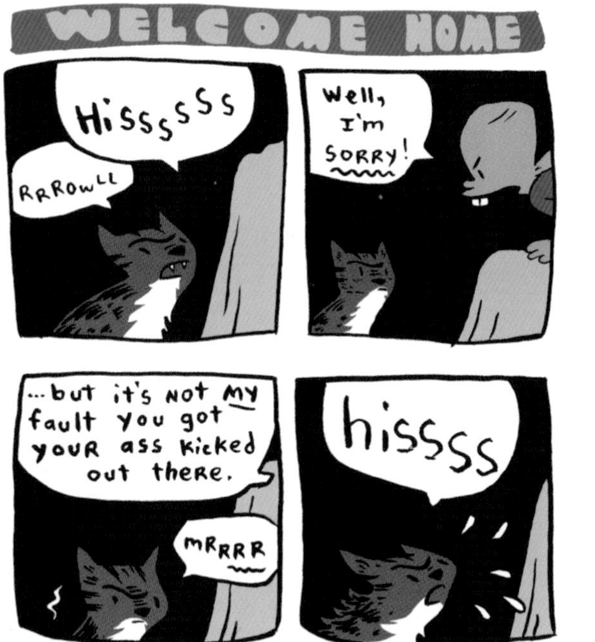
WELCOME HOME
HissssSs
RRROWLL
Well, I'm SORRY!
...but it's not MY fault you got your ass kicked out there.
mRRRR
hissss
AUGUST 5, 2004

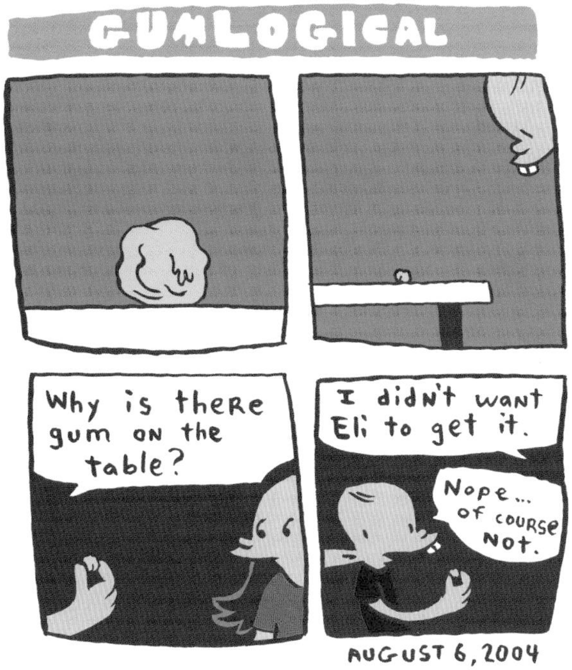
GUMLOGICAL
Why is there gum on the table?
I didn't want Eli to get it.
Nope... of course not.
AUGUST 6, 2004

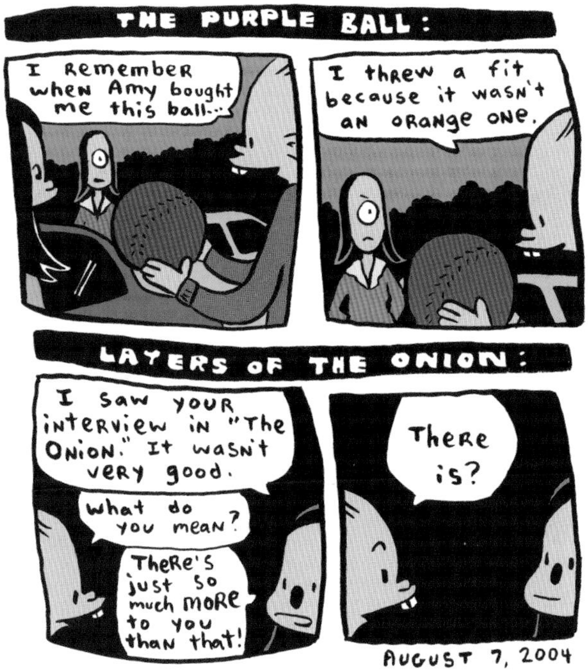
THE PURPLE BALL:
I remember when Amy bought me this ball...
I threw a fit because it wasn't an orange one.
LAYERS OF THE ONION:
I saw your interview in "The Onion." It wasn't very good.
What do you mean?
There's just so much more to you than that!
There is?
AUGUST 7, 2004

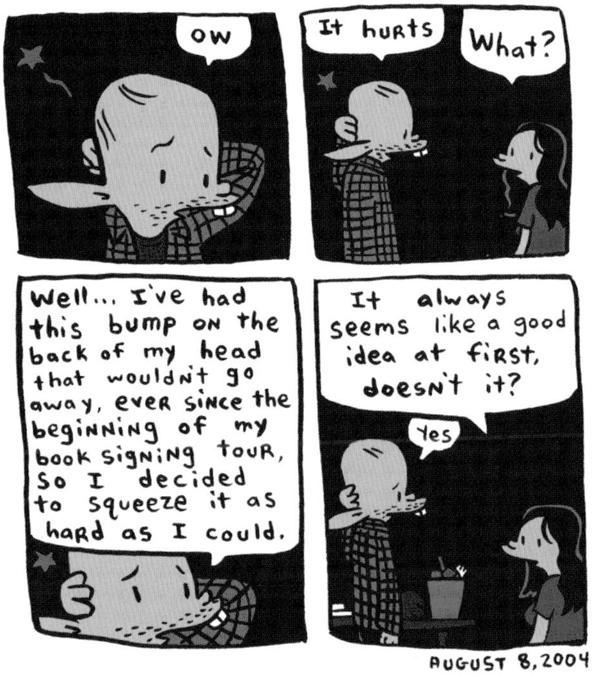
OW
It hurts
What?
Well... I've had this bump on the back of my head that wouldn't go away, ever since the beginning of my book signing tour, so I decided to squeeze it as hard as I could.
It always seems like a good idea at first, doesn't it?
Yes
AUGUST 8, 2004

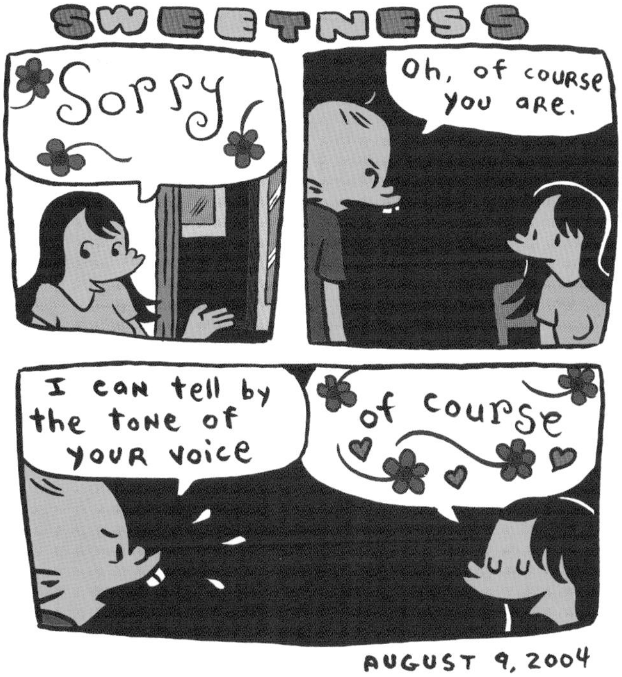
SWEETNESS
Sorry
Oh, of course you are.
I can tell by the tone of your voice
of course
AUGUST 9, 2004

LONG BANGS

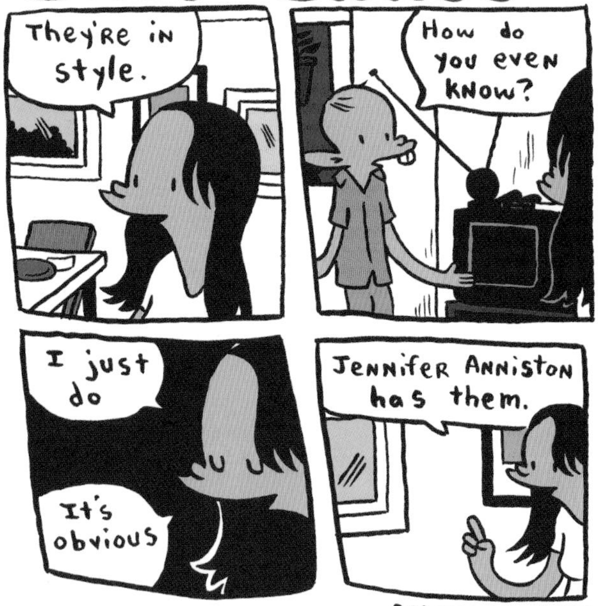
They're in style.
How do you even know?
I just do
It's obvious
Jennifer Anniston has them.

AUGUST 10, 2004

PLAY IT COOL

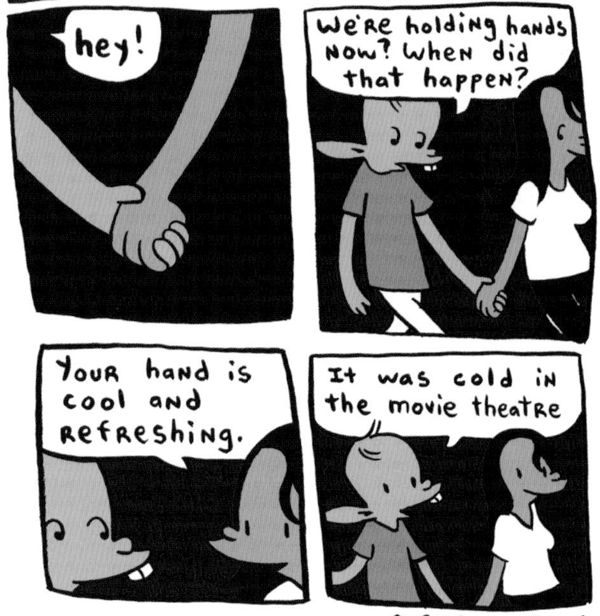
hey!
We're holding hands now? When did that happen?
Your hand is cool and refreshing.
It was cold in the movie theatre

AUGUST 11, 2004

FAMILY DROOL

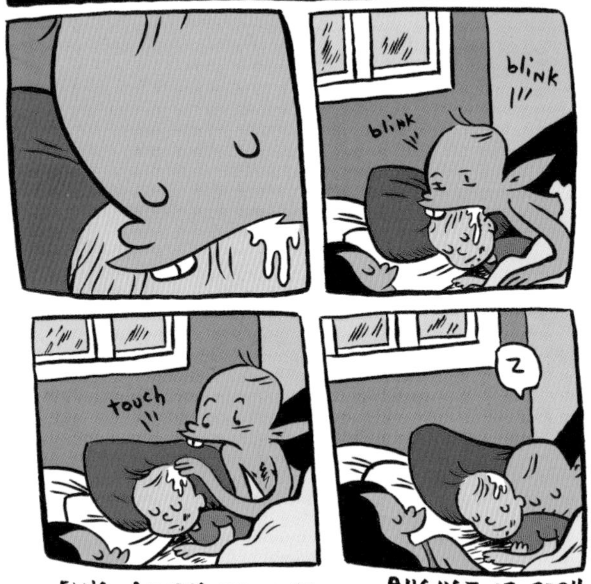
blink
blink
touch
z

ELI'S ALWAYS DROOLING ON ME... SO TURNABOUT IS FAIR PLAY!

AUGUST 12, 2004

WORRY WORLD

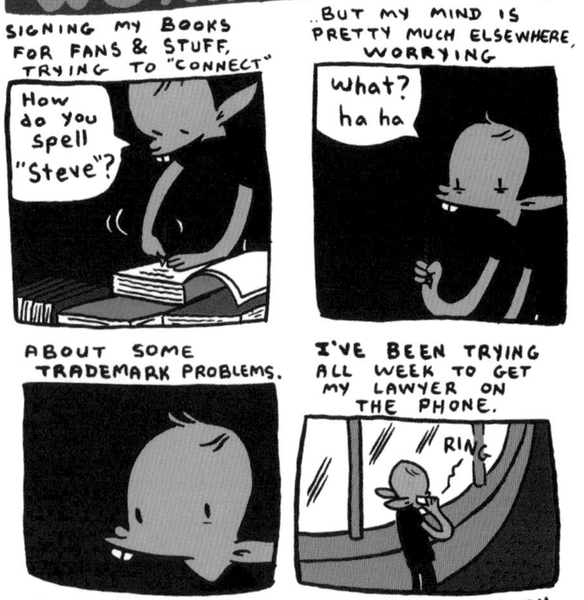
SIGNING MY BOOKS FOR FANS & STUFF, TRYING TO "CONNECT"
How do you spell "Steve"?
..BUT MY MIND IS PRETTY MUCH ELSEWHERE, WORRYING
What? ha ha
ABOUT SOME TRADEMARK PROBLEMS.
I'VE BEEN TRYING ALL WEEK TO GET MY LAWYER ON THE PHONE.
RING

WIZARD WORLD, CHICAGO

AUGUST 13, 2004

I'M JAMES KOCHALKA

Oh, man it's GREAT to meet you! I LOVE your work

Thank you

Yeah, I just LOVED "Box office Poison"!

!!

Box Office Poison is by Alex Robinson.

I'm James Kochalka

Oh... Well... I love your work too

No you don't

WIZARD WORLD, CHICAGO: AUGUST 14, 2004

♥ THE FAM BAM

WAAAAA

WAA

Eli's been crying a lot for stupid reasons

That's so cute. I LOVE you guys!

CALLING FROM WAYNE'S IN CHICAGO

AUGUST 15, 2004

I FEEL FAMOUS

AFTER MY TOUR, I FEEL FAMOUS.

I'M TINGLING WITH CONFIDENCE IN MY POWERS AND ACCOMPLISHMENTS.

I AM A MAN,

NOT A WEIRD BALDING CHILD.

SPLASH

AUGUST 16, 2004

DON'T WORRY

IT WAS A SUNNY DAY SO I GOT UP ON THE ROOF AND WORKED ON PAINTING THE TRIM.

I WORKED, AND DIDN'T WORRY ABOUT MY BOOK RELEASE PARTY TONIGHT AT CROW BOOKSHOP.

WHEN THE DOORS OPENED AT CROW ONLY A VERY FEW PEOPLE WERE WAITING TO GET IN... I SET UPON SIGNING & SKETCHING IN THEIR BOOKS.

So... what's your name?

WHEN I LOOKED UP AGAIN, THE PLACE WAS PACKED

WOAH!

AUGUST 17, 2004

OPERATION HAPPY BIRTHDAY

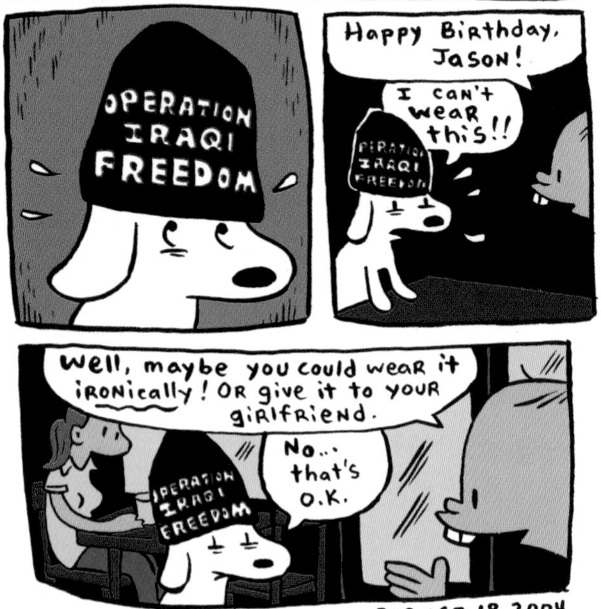
OPERATION IRAQI FREEDOM
Happy Birthday, Jason!
I can't wear this!!
OPERATION IRAQI FREEDOM
Well, maybe you could wear it ironically! Or give it to your girlfriend.
No... that's O.K.
OPERATION IRAQI FREEDOM

AUGUST 18, 2004

THE THINKER

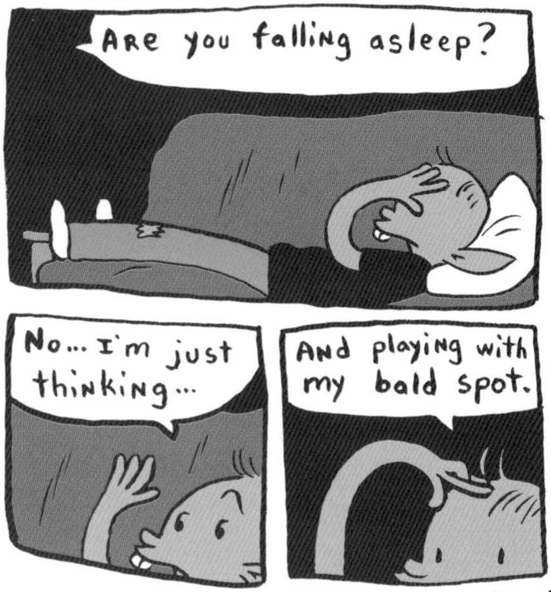
Are you falling asleep?
No... I'm just thinking...
And playing with my bald spot.

AUGUST 19, 2004

LI'L SKETCHY BOOK-BOOK

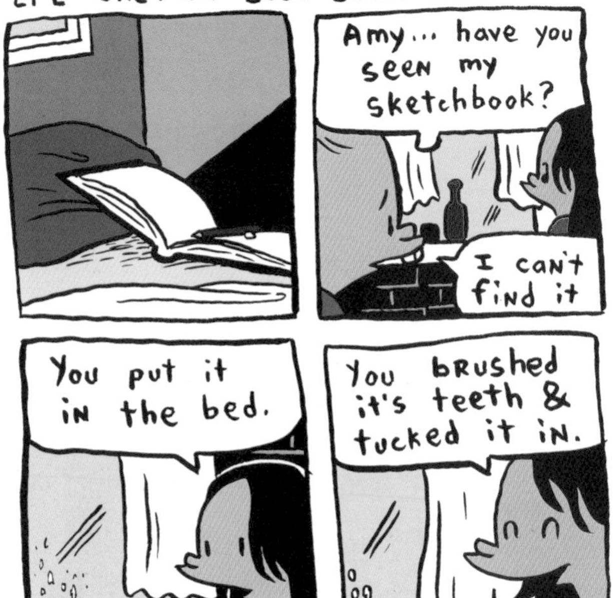
Amy... have you seen my sketchbook?
I can't find it
You put it in the bed.
You brushed it's teeth & tucked it in.

AUGUST 20, 2004

BIRTHDAY BOY JOY

A QUIET MOMENT BEFORE THE GUESTS SHOW UP:

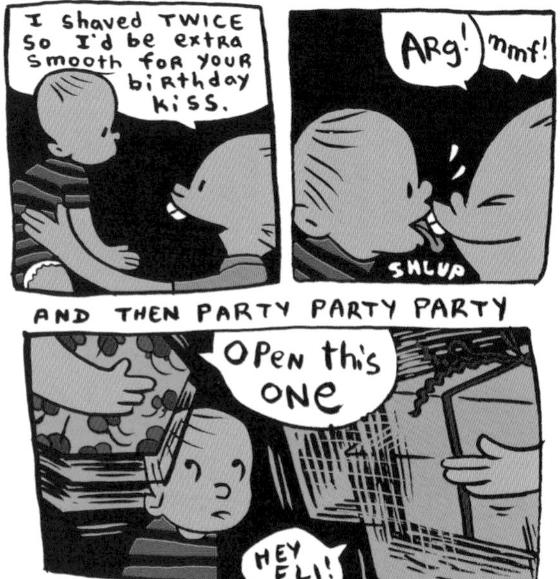
I shaved TWICE so I'd be extra smooth for your birthday kiss.
ARG!
mmf!
SHLUP
AND THEN PARTY PARTY PARTY
OPen this ONE
HEY ELI!

AUGUST 21, 2004

DIAGNOSIS

My face hurts

Maybe it's your hypochondria acting up.

BEDTIME SCIENCE

Babies can't sleep standing up.

It violates the 3rd Law of Babydynamics!

AUGUST 22, 2004

LUCKY CRACKER

James, LOOK!

OH MY GOD!

his lucky CRACKER gave him the power to walk!

AUGUST 23, 2004

A BRIEF REPRIEVE?

You're in a better mood today.

Yeah

Today no one sent me mean emails about how much everyone hates me.

BABY MAN

but I think Eli gave me his cold...

ahem

But you can handle it better than a baby, right?

AUGUST 24, 2004

SORE ACHE

My throat hurts

My ear aches.

Let me see

OW! NO

It aches!

Maybe you've got an earache.

Maybe you've got a sorethroat!

AUGUST 25, 2004

THE REASON

blech!

For some reason my face feels all slimey.

Ah! For some reason my hair hurts.

AUGUST 26, 2004

MUTANT

JOE!

come here

A two headed ant!

I never saw a 2-headed ant before.

It's a mutANT!

AUGUST 27, 2004

HOT BUTTERED

Remember when I used to put butter in my coffee?

That never really caught on.

tink tink

You said it tasted like pussy

heh heh hee

AUGUST 28, 2004

RAINED

It's raining HARD! I better go upstairs and shut the windows.

AUGUST 29, 2004

THE PAJAMAFICATION OF AMERICA

I changed my mind... don't write about the Pajamafication of America.

What?! Why not?

It's my idea, I want to use it myself.

But the phrase has already entered my vernacular! It's too late

SORRY TOM!

AUGUST 30, 2004

YOU'D LIKE HIM

Right now I'm looking at a frog.

Oh, he's sleek and beautiful!

Green with black spots.

You'd like him.

AUGUST 31, 2004

THE FURTHER ADVENTURES OF
PINKY & STINKY

Remember how I sold the television rights in my book Pinky & Stinky, but it didn't work out and they gave it back? We'll I found another company to sell the rights to.

Oh! That's GREAT!!!!

Well... but I love all my characters so much...

It kind of feels like I'm selling them into SLAVERY.

SEPTEMBER 1, 2004

I'M SOMEONE

TUG

CLICK

"Someone" left the light on in the basement.

SEPTEMBER 2, 2004

PRECARIOUS

what the FUCK am I doing up here

I don't like the look of how that ladder is set up.. *

* VOICE OF THE NEIGHBOR

If you put too much weight at the top –

–Yeah, it'll flip up, I know!!

but I don't weigh too much.

SEPTEMBER 3, 2004

WINE AND THE FRONT DOOR

ALAN LEFT THE FRONT DOOR OPEN WHEN HE WENT TO GET MORE WINE.

SPANDY GOT OUT...

FOLLOWED BY ELI!!!

The end

SEPTEMBER 4, 2004

SEVERAL TIMES A NIGHT, ELI SPONTANEOUSLY SITS UP IN HIS SLEEP:

WAAA

SEPTEMBER 5, 2004

A DELICIOUS STORY, SIMPLY TOLD:

PANCAKES

I want pancakes.

BEEP BEEP BOOP

Hey, how about we come over and you make us pancakes?

O.K?

GREAT

That was easy!

Amy!

We're going to Alan & Trixie's for pancakes

SEPTEMBER 6, 2004

THE RUSH of LOVE

AMY AND I HAVE BEEN TOGETHER SINCE 1986. ONE DAY CAME THE REALIZATION THAT I'D PROBABLY NEVER FALL IN LOVE WITH SOMEONE EVER AGAIN, NEVER FEEL THAT RUSH OF JOY. HOWEVER, I WAS WRONG. I'VE FALLEN IN LOVE WITH AMY AGAIN AND AGAIN, MANY TIMES OVER.

AND THEN I FELL IN LOVE WITH OUR BABY!

hyeah hyeah ha ha hee!

RaR!

SEPTEMBER 7, 2004

SMALL VILLE

I TURN OFF THE T.V.

ZORP

...AND I HEAR THAT AMY IS WATCHING THE SAME SHOW UPSTAIRS.

I thought you were asleep.

I thought I was too.

SEPTEMBER 8, 2004

THE PASSING OF THE DAYS:

SEPTEMBER NINE

I'm toooo tired. I'll just draw today's strip tomorrow.

That's not cheating

SEPTEMBER TEN

I don't remember a single thing that happened yesterday.

SEPTEMBER 9 & 10, 2004

TALKIN' TRASH

IT'S TWO O'CLOCK A.M.

This stupid clock doesn't work. I'm throwing it out.

IT'S ELEVEN O'CLOCK P.M.

The trash just told me the time

SEPTEMBER 10, 2004

LAST NIGHT AT CHRIS & KATE'S WEDDING
LOVE BOATS ON HEWITT LAKE

My pirate boat is gonna sink the other boats

SEPTEMBER 11, 2004

YESTERDAY'S
WEDDING REGATTA

SNAP

What happened?!!

The mast SNAPPED!

DRAWN SEPTEMBER 12, 2004

SLOW DOWN

FLAP
FLAP FLAP
FLAP
FLAP FLAP

You just barely learned how to walk and ALREADY you're trying to learn to fly?!!

FLAP FLAP

SEPTEMBER 13, 2004

FUN WITH JASON

Put Eli on the phone

... I want to be the first PERSON to ever hang up on him.

Eli, it's Jason.

?

CLICK !!!

SEPTEMBER 14, 2004

SEPTEMBER 15, 2004

SEPTEMBER 16, 2004

SEPTEMBER 17, 2004

SEPTEMBER 18, 2004

SEPTEMBER 19, 2004

"THE CURIOUS INCIDENT OF THE DOG IN THE NIGHT-TIME"

SEPTEMBER 20, 2004

SEPTEMBER 21, 2004

SEPTEMBER 22, 2004

P.H.O.

Do you want some snacks?

Yes, without PHO's, please

What are P-H-O s?

Partially Hydrogenated Oils

So... what's WRONG with them? They're NOT as good as fully hydrogenated ones?

NO

Yeah, either fully hydrogenate or get off the pot!

SEPTEMBER 23, 2004

SPINNING

LIFE RUSHES BY.

I CAN'T DRAW FAST ENOUGH TO KEEP UP.

creak

SEPTEMBER 24, 2004

LENNY'S FUNERAL

GULP

— TREMBLE

— QUIVER

...So, one day he came up to me in the school library and said "James, hit me in the forehead as hard as you can."

So I hit him in the forehead as hard as I could.

He said "Thanks!" and RAN away...

Ha ha ha Ha ha ha

SEPTEMBER 25, 2004

RASPBERRY FROG

I WAS DIGGING A HOLE TO PLANT RASPBERRIES IN.

I NOTICED A FRESHLY DEAD FROG WITH HIS GUTS SQUISHED OUT.

I must've stepped on him and not even known it.

SO I BURIED HIM WITH THE ROOTS OF THE RASPBERRY PLANTS.

SEPTEMBER 26, 2004

NIGHT BIKE

I've pushed the baby stroller down this sidewalk so many times...

...I know where all the bumps are, even in the dark

eek

BUMP

SEPTEMBER 27, 2004

SPIKEY

So, I guess croquet is all the rage now?

Oh yes!

Do you know what else all the rage?

What?

Spiking your hair up with raspberry yogurt

SEPTEMBER 28, 2004

EASILY DISCOMBOBULATED

I like this model, ...the "Roxbury"

That's a nice futon frame

We won't have any of those til the end of October

Oh

ALL MY PLANS ARE THROWN IN DISARRAY

Is there another model you like?

I feel dizzy

SEPTEMBER 29, 2004

ELECTION 2004
BEFORE THE DEBATE

IN CHRIS & KATE'S APARTMENT IN WASHINGTON, DC, THE FUTURE OF THE WORLD HANGS IN THE BALANCE:

AFTER THE DEBATE

There's definitely too much conditioner in my hair

SEPTEMBER 30, 2004

Holiday Inn SELECT Bethesda

It's 12:30 ?! I've got work to do! I've still got to draw today's diary strip!

Wait... it's not in my bag? That means I left my sketchbook locked in the convention hall..

Well, I've got a pen in my pocket. Maybe I could find some paper here with the hotel insignia or something.

That would be perfect

OCTOBER 1, 2004
AT THE SMALL PRESS EXPO

FREE DRINK TICKETS

Do you want a drink ticket?

SURE!

I've already got enough drink tickets to drink myself to death!

OCTOBER 2, 2004

IGNATZ AWARDS

Geez, James. Your acceptence speech was AWFUL!

Yes, it was bad

Well... I got NERVOUS...

Tsk Tsk Tsk

I panicked

and the ignatz goes to...

AT THE VERY END OF THE AWARDS CEREMONY, I JUMPED UP AND GAVE A SECOND TRY AT MY SPEECH:

It was just stupid!

AT THE SMALL PRESS EXPO, OCTOBER 3, 2004

RISE ABOVE

Your flight is delayed

KATE

ABRAHAM LINCOLN

MM

OLD NEW GUY

Do you want to go back to wait at Kate's?

Who knows ...it could be delayed even longer

Oh... I think I'll just stick to my original plans... even if the airline doesn't.

OCTOBER 4, 2004
WASHINGTON, DC

SPANDY HURT HER PAW WHILE I WAS GONE.

IT MAKES HER EASIER TO CHASE:

OCTOBER 5, 2004

OCTOBER 6, 2004

THE OBJECT

SOMETIMES IT FEELS LIKE SOMETHING HUGE IS FLOATING JUST BEHIND MY HEAD.

OCTOBER 7, 2004

OCTOBER 8, 2004

SHUFFLING THROUGH

SHUF
SHUF

Maybe you can find a TICK

OCTOBER 9, 2004

BEFORE CLEANING THE HOUSE,
BUT OF COURSE!

Would you like a glass of wine?

Sure, why not

It is eleven-thirty in the morning, after all!

OCTOBER 10, 2004

DON'T TAKE HIM

Come on, Sweetie

Noɒo

I forgot he had daycare today—

OCTOBER 11, 2004

HOORAY FOR ROOFING

If you climb up you can see the big rotten spot I found in your roof.

oh yeah?

hooray!

OCTOBER 12, 2004

MY BROTHER-IN-LAW AND MY NEPHEW AND A FRIEND OF THEIRS HAVE ALL MOVED INTO OUR HOUSE FOR THE WEEK WHILE THEY PUT ON OUR NEW ROOF.

Hey, Joe. We want to come to your party tomorrow.

But if we do, we'll have to bring our guests along probably

My...um... my brother-in-law is kind of scary looking

but he's nice

LATER Oh! I should've told Joe about how my nephew plugged up the toilet.

OCTOBER 13, 2004

NO GOING

BEFORE KELLY'S PRE-GOING AWAY PARTY

I don't think friends should move away.

LATER, AT KELLY'S ACTUAL PARTY *

I think we should have a rule that friends aren't allowed to move away.

OCTOBER 14, 2004

* KELLY & JOE'S & NINA'S

OCTOBER 15, 2004

REGRET

I wish I could go back and be nicer to you every day I've known you.

You could just be nicer to me every day in the future.

That sounds too hard.

OCTOBER 16, 2004

OCTOBER 17, 2004

OCTOBER 18, 2004

OCTOBER 19, 2004

OCTOBER 20, 2004

THE SHOCK OF AWAKING

blink blink

Eli doesn't have a HEAD!

Oh

OCTOBER 21, 2004

GOLD CEILINGS & CHANDELIERS

CRESTON TRIED to get us a show here once, but the guy said "I don't think people want to hear you sing about your dick while drinking eight dollar glasses of wine."

Well, that guy doesn't work here anymore

My glass of wine cost TEN dollars!

OCTOBER 22, 2004

GIG MONEY

I just wanted to be sure you understood why I split the money the way we did.

Splitting it up by musician is more fair because each musician did the same amount of "work"

What?

It is?!

Happy birthday, Colin.

OCTOBER 23, 2004

SUBSCRIPTION

Being married is like having a subscription to Playboy...

...except every month the centerfold is the same girl.

And every month she gets more beautiful?

Yup

OCTOBER 24, 2004

In celebration of the haircut you got last friday, I'm going to draw your portrait

O.K.

OCTOBER 25, 2004

HIS MOTHER'S BOOTS

ha ha

He's getting good at playing by himself.

Yes, but he has spots on his face

OCTOBER 26, 2004

GOOD TUB TIME

That looks FUN!

Splash

I'm coming in!

SPLASH

OCTOBER 27, 2004

TRIGGED BY TELEVISION

TRIGGERED BY SOMETHING I SAW ON TELEVISION I WAS SUDDENLY FLOODED WITH MEMORIES FROM THE DAY OF ELI'S BIRTH.

THE INTENSITY OF EMOTION WAS ALMOST TOO MUCH TO BEAR.

OCTOBER 28, 2004

ANTIMATTER

There's an interesting mix of adults and college students here

Yeah... it's amazing the place doesn't EXPLODE

OCTOBER 29, 2004

RRRICH

I think I forgot to brush my teeth today...

SNIF

hmm

very Rich!

OCTOBER 30, 2004

ELI, THE THREE HEADED BEAR

YOUR COSTUME SUCKS

James Kochalka!

Fuck YEAH

Oh, wait... I know who you're supposed to be!

Oh yeah?

HALLOWEEN, OCTOBER 31, 2004

OPTIMISTIC

I guess we can relax...

BUSH won't be president much longer now.

FOUR MORE YEARS, TOPS.

that!

ha

NOVEMBER 1, 2004

BONK THE VOTE

MY NEEDS. WANTS. AND FEARS.

MY VOTE

BONK BONK

Honey... don't bonk your head on the voting booth.

Ha Ha

BONK

NOVEMBER 2, 2004

OUTSIDE THE WINDOW IT IS GRAY AND COLD.

THERE'S BAD NEWS ON THE TELEVISION...

Bush

BUT MY LITTLE BOY IS BEAMING.

NOVEMBER 3, 2004

MY FELLOW MAN

The sky looks like a watercolor

OR ink wash

And the air smells like curry!

The air smells strongly of curry. don't you think?

Yeah? Fuck you!

(YESTERDAY)

NOVEMBER 4, 2004

A STREETLIGHT & SEVERAL HOUSES FORMED THIS STAR:

NOV. 5, 2004

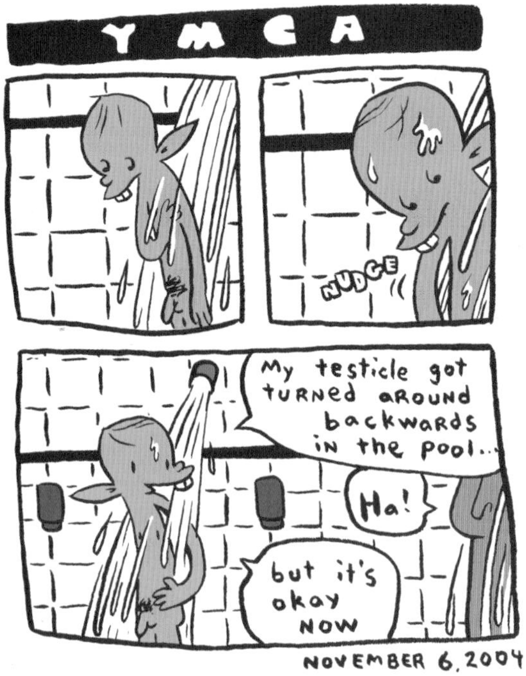
YMCA
NUDGE
My testicle got turned around backwards in the pool...
Ha!
but it's okay now
NOVEMBER 6, 2004

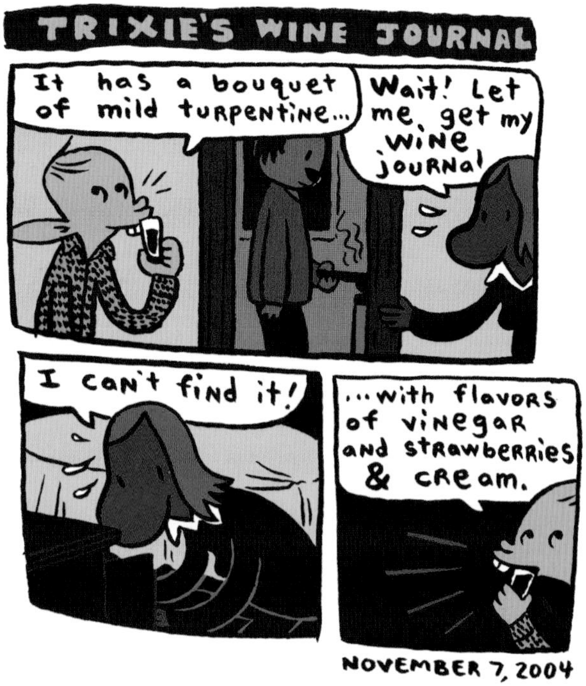
TRIXIE'S WINE JOURNAL
It has a bouquet of mild turpentine...
Wait! Let me get my wine journal
I can't find it!
...with flavors of vinegar and strawberries & cream.
NOVEMBER 7, 2004

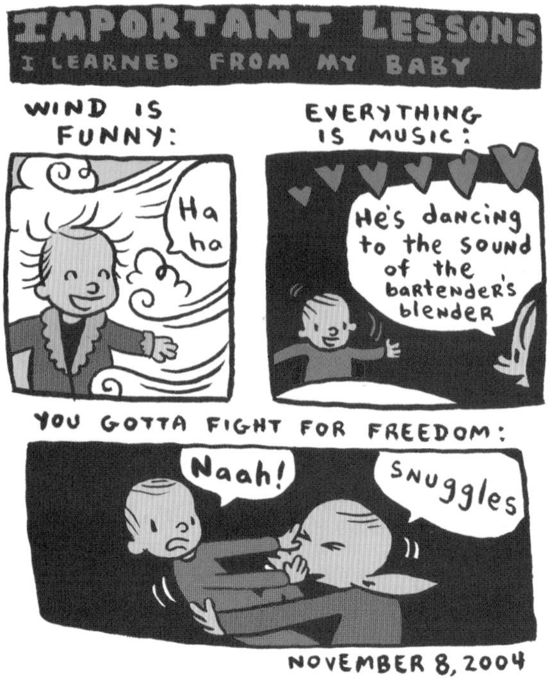
IMPORTANT LESSONS
I LEARNED FROM MY BABY
WIND IS FUNNY:
Ha ha
EVERYTHING IS MUSIC:
He's dancing to the sound of the bartender's blender
YOU GOTTA FIGHT FOR FREEDOM:
Naah!
Snuggles
NOVEMBER 8, 2004

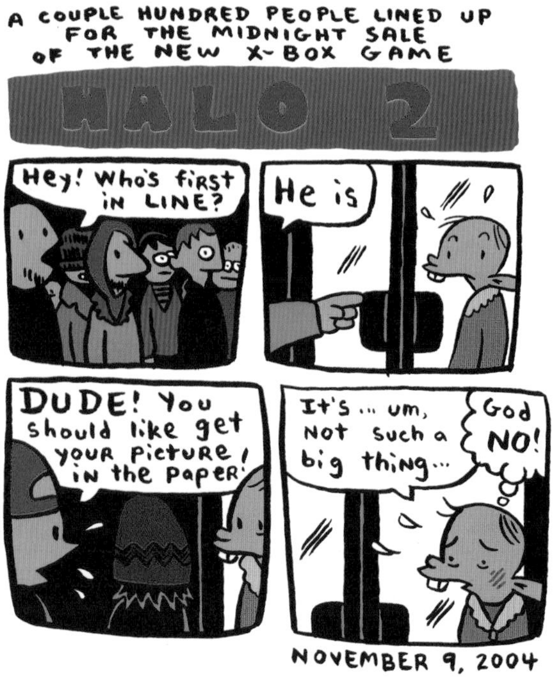
A COUPLE HUNDRED PEOPLE LINED UP FOR THE MIDNIGHT SALE OF THE NEW X-BOX GAME
HALO 2
Hey! Who's first in LINE?
He is
DUDE! You should like get your picture in the paper!
It's... um, not such a big thing...
God NO!
NOVEMBER 9, 2004

WE ARE TIRED

By my count, Eli woke up nineteen times last night.

blah blah blah

NOVEMBER 10, 2004

MY BURDEN

Let this be a lesson to you!

"Don't yell"? "Be nice"? "Be a good person"?

No!

Don't stay up all night playing video games!

NOVEMBER 11, 2004

WHAT ARE WE DOING TONIGHT?

Are we looking at our titties in the mirror?

No... kitty kicked me in the chest and scratched me.

NOVEMBER 12, 2004

FRIEND WANTED

Now that Kelly is moving away...

Who will replace her position in your comic strip?

huh?

You should totally hold auditions!

Ha!

NOVEMBER 13, 2004

JONATHAN RICHMAN

He looks twice as old as the last time I saw him.

He's probably thinking the same thing about you!

NOVEMBER 14, 2004

THOSE HILARIOUS RIB CRACKERS

I think I cracked a rib while we were making love this weekend.

No you didn't.

harumph

Well, I didn't crack it jerking off!

God!

NOVEMBER 15, 2004

TOOTHBRUSH FIGHTERS

RRAR!

Mewr!

NOVEMBER 16, 2004

THREE FOR KELLY

This is the third going away party for Kelly I've been to.

I think I've only been to two...

I've been to three

Tonight's, last Saturday's, and one about a month ago or something.

Oh! Then I've been to three, too!

NATE

NOVEMBER 17, 2004

CRAZY LOGZ

All our new firewood is growing MOLDY. Is that NORMAL?

NOVEMBER 18, 2004

SURPRISE

AT MY P.O. BOX I GOT A COOL LETTER FROM FRED SCHNEIDER OF THE B-52'S:

Ooh!

AT HOME I GOT THE FINAL COPY OF THE CONTRACT FOR THE NEW PINKY & STINKY TELEVISION DEAL:

Another Surprise

WE WENT OUT TO EAT AT THE CHINESE RESTAURANT WHERE I HAD WORKED FOR SIX LONG YEARS:

THEN WHEN I GOT BACK HOME, I THREW UP:

GLURK

NOVEMBER 19, 2004

CAT LICKED BUTTER

The cat's definitely been licking this butter

But that's okay. Nothing tastes better than cat-licked butter on toast!

CRUNCH

NOVEMBER 20, 2004

OILED SQUEAKERS

Do the wheels still squeak?

Nope!

Nothing oils squeaky wheels better than cat-licked butter!

I used WD-40

ha!

NOVEMBER 21, 2004

LITTLE GAMER

ELI LIKES TO PUSH BUTTONS ON THE X-BOX CONTROLLER WHILE HE WATCHES T.V.

IT LOOKS FUN!

Da!

NOVEMBER 22, 2004

$25.00 WINE IS BETTER THAN $8.00 WINE

IN THE MAGIC REALM

I TURNED THE HOUSE UPSIDE DOWN LOOKING FOR MY PASSPORT. IT TURNED OUT IT WAS HIDDEN IN A ROLLED UP TRAVEL BAG, UNDER SOME BLANKETS, AT THE BOTTOM OF THE BASKET THAT SPANDY LIKES TO SLEEP IN, IN THE CLOSET.

THE FAERIES WON'T WAVE THEIR MAGIC WANDS OVER THE SECRET DOCUMENTS IF YOU DON'T HAVE A PASSPORT.

KA-CHUNK

IT'S THE ONLY WAY TO BE INVITED IN TO THEIR MAGIC REALM. CELEBRATE WITH EXPENSIVE WINE.

I wonder if we can tell the difference.

Wow!

NOVEMBER 23, 2004

GRANDPA & GRANDMA'S

There's dust all over my sweater.

There's dust all over the baby!

Aah-choo!

THE UNIVERSE WILL ONE DAY SUFFOCATE UNDER THE WEIGHT OF IT'S OWN DUST.

NOVEMBER 24, 2004

DUSTY THANKSGIVING

HAPPY DUSTGIVING

Have my eyes blistered from the dust?

Cough Cough Cough

My lungs are shutting down.

AT MY PARENT'S HOUSE, NOVEMBER 25, 2004

DUST TO DUST

MY PARENTS ARE GETTING VERY OLD. TIME IS SLOWING DOWN. THE PILES OF JUNK ARE GETTING DEEPER.

THE COFFEE MY FATHER MAKES TASTES LIKE IT WAS BREWED FROM DUST AND DEAD MOTHS.

AMY AND I LAUGH ABOUT IT.

BUT I FEEL BAD. MY PARENTS ARE SLOWLY TURNING TO DUST.

It's insane!
hee hee

NOVEMBER 26, 2004

EVERYTHING WAS FINE UNTIL THE OLD

WAKEY WAKE

WAAAAA

AAAA

James... can you help Eli go back to sleep?

wha-?
WAAA
Uh... No...
I don't think I can

AAAA
why not?!
I think I'm going to throw up

NOVEMBER 27, 2004

LACTOSE INTOLERANCE

I didn't drink any alcohol

Why do I feel like this?

Sort of hung over like.

Maybe from all the eggnog & milk you drank

Yeah, I'm hungover from FARTING!

NOVEMBER 28, 2004

ALL MY BIG IDEAS...

Zounds

What an idea!

...TEND TO SHRINK UPON EXECUTION.

That's it?

(AND THE LITTLE IDEAS GET BIGGER)

NOVEMBER 29, 2004

FAILURE OF THE ELVES

They didn't take our recycling.

They took all the neighbors' recycling but not ours.

Maybe I did it wrong.

NOVEMBER 30, 2004

FAT EYE

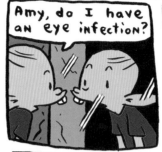

Amy, do I have an eye infection?

It's hard to tell because I have naturally fat eyes.

If it spreads to me and Eli, then we'll know.

DECEMBER 1, 2004

OH, SNAPSHOT

Yay! Clickity clack

Amy! Let me take your picture. Take off your hat!

umm

Can you try to look a little prettier?

My stomach hurts

but I'll try

DECEMBER 2, 2004

SNOWWALKING

He thinks that because it's snowing, he can't move!

It's not true, Eli! You can go anywhere you want. Look!

La La La

SHUF

DECEMBER 3, 2004

MY GREAT OLD COLLEGE FRIEND DERRICK CALLED.

James! Telephone!

CLUNK

WE TALKED FOR ABOUT AN HOUR.

Ha ha ha

MEANWHILE, I KEPT ON DRAWING. GOTTA GET STUFF DONE.

uh huh

oh yeah?

mm-hmm

I FELT A LI'L GUILTY WHEN I LOST THE THREAD OF THE CONVERSATION.

Wait...

what? ??

DECEMBER 4, 2004

TRANSLATION

I THINK NEXT YEAR MY DIARY WILL FINALLY BE PUBLISHED IN FRENCH

?

Eli has bear feet but he doesn't have bare feet!

If I drew this as a strip how would they translate it?

Would it still rhyme?*

And all the idiomatic expressions of my own invention!

It's impossibobble!

DECEMBER 5, 2004

* RHYME IS NOT THE WORD I'M LOOKING FOR

WATER & STEAM

I like sharing a glass of water with Amy, after we make love

SLUP

Aah!

VISION OF LAST SATURDAY

DECEMBER 6, 2004

D.S. B.S.

ON Saturday you said if I pre-paid for a "Nintendo DS", I could pick it up today.

HALF LIFE2   DOOM 3

Well, I said there were no guarantees

Actually NO

That's NOT what you said at all

HALF LIFE2

Well, I don't know what I said!!

HALF LIFE2

GEEZ! I'm going to QUIT this stupid job!

Sorry, Spandy. I couldn't get your Nintendo DS

* DUAL-SCREEN BULL-SHIT

DECEMBER 7, 2004

ATTACK OF THE MONSTER

My feet are a Monster!

RAR!

My feet are eating your BOTTOM!

Ha ha

DECEMBER 8, 2004

TICKLE TWITCH

MY EYE STARTED TO TICKLE & FEEL WEIRD.

TWITCH

SO I BLINKED IT AS HARD AS I COULD:

THAT HURT!

!!!

DECEMBER 9, 2004

BEFORE & AFTER

MY HAIRCUT HAPPENED SO QUICK,

I THOUGHT THAT I MIGHT CRY.

Are you in shock?

LATER

It looks good, but you don't look just like ELI anymore

12/10/04

BEFORE

AFTER

WATCHING IT HAPPEN IN LAND OF FOG & SNOW

I WATCHED A BALLOON DISAPPEAR INTO THE FOG & SNOW:

LATER

Do you like going bald? Do you like growing older?

Yes

It's pretty fun

DECEMBER 11, 2004

15 MINUTES IN THE MALL

That wasn't 15 minutes! That was an HOUR!

I bought you some nice presents

Phhff! I don't want 'em

DECEMBER 12, 2004

HEATSEEKER

(ON THE GRATE LIKE A LI'L MARILYN MONROE

DECEMBER 13, 2004

I HAVE TOO MUCH DRAWING I PROMISED I'D DO! ELI WOULDN'T TAKE A NAP AND I FELL INTO A DIZZYING SPIRAL OF ANGRY DESPAIR

STRIKING MYSELF TWICE IN THE FACE. I'M NOT SURE HOW THIS HAPPENED

SMACK SNAP

WUMP

SLAMMING THE REFRIGERATOR DOOR & BREAKING IT

EVERYTHING FELL OUT

"SPIRAL OF DESPAIR" 12/14/04

EPOXY

I fixed the REFRIGERATOR DOOR...

I'd feel more PROUD of myself if I waSN't So embarrassed of how I broke it.

We're PROUD of you!

SUCK

DECEMBER 15, 2004

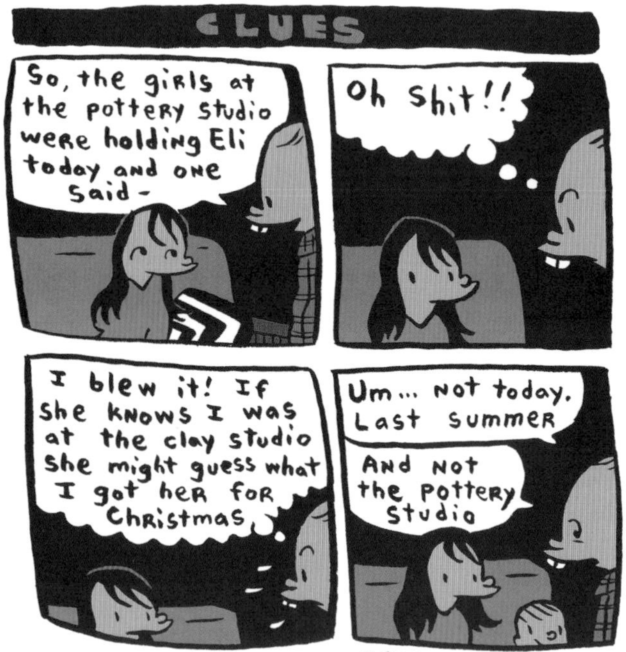
CLUES
So, the girls at the pottery studio were holding Eli today and one said-
Oh Shit!!
I blew it! If she knows I was at the clay studio she might guess what I got her for Christmas.
Um... not today. Last summer
And not the pottery studio

DECEMBER 16, 2004

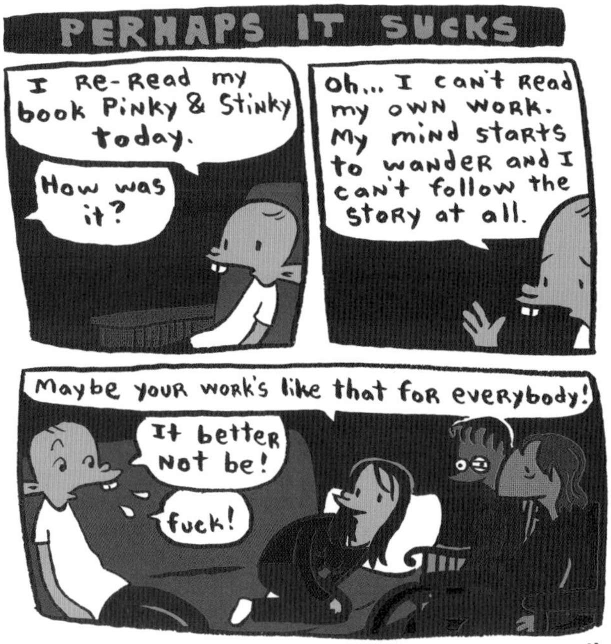
PERHAPS IT SUCKS
I re-read my book Pinky & Stinky today.
How was it?
Oh... I can't read my own work. My mind starts to wander and I can't follow the story at all.
Maybe your work's like that for everybody!
It better not be!
fuck!

DECEMBER 17, 2004

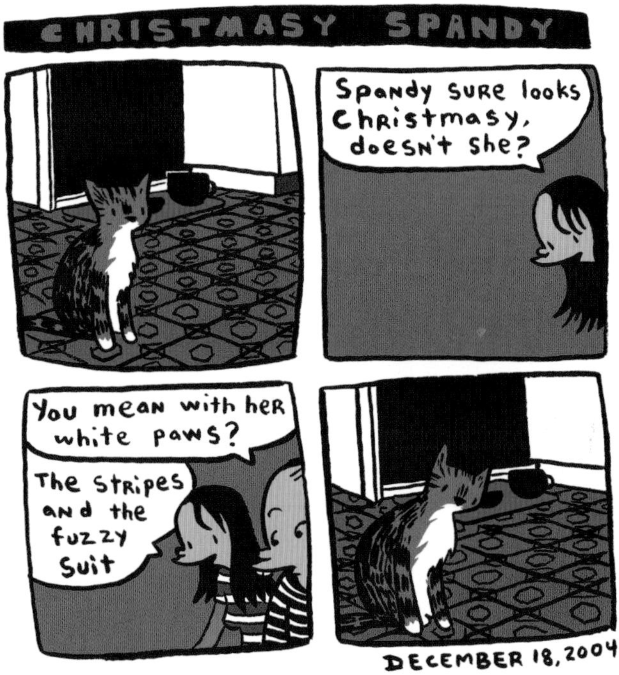
CHRISTMASY SPANDY
Spandy sure looks Christmasy, doesn't she?
You mean with her white paws?
The stripes and the fuzzy suit

DECEMBER 18, 2004

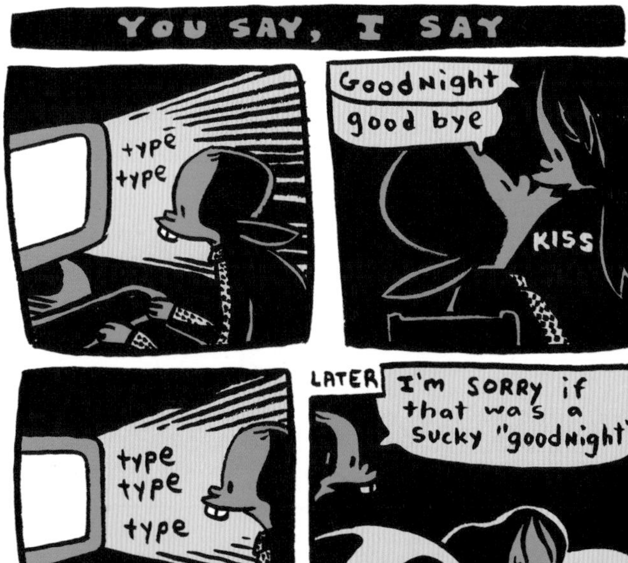
YOU SAY, I SAY
type type
Goodnight
good bye
KISS
type type type
LATER
I'm sorry if that was a sucky "goodnight"

DECEMBER 19, 2004

WINTER WALK

COLD LIKE NEEDLES IN MY FACE.

WOW! IT FEELS LIKE MY NOSE IS BEING SPLIT OPEN DOWN THE MIDDLE FROM THE INSIDE!

LATER

So... I was just walking along minding my own business when this guy stops to tell me my nose is starting to frostbite!

Was it turning white?

DECEMBER 20, 2004

SNOWSUIT WIGGLER

Eli!

WAA

Stop wiggling and get in your SNOWSUIT!

ERmf!

Whoops! You've got one leg in a leg hole and one in an arm hole!

DECEMBER 21, 2004

BEAUTY SORES

Who will be the prettiest boy at the Christmas Party?

You?

Even though you have sores on your face?

He'll be the prettiest BECAUSE he has sores!

That's Right! They're BEAUTY SORES!

DECEMBER 22, 2004

DRIVING HOME FROM MY ROCK SHOW RIGHT INTO A

BLACK HOLE

That's a weird sign.

I think it means we're heading into a black hole.

DECEMBER 23, 2004

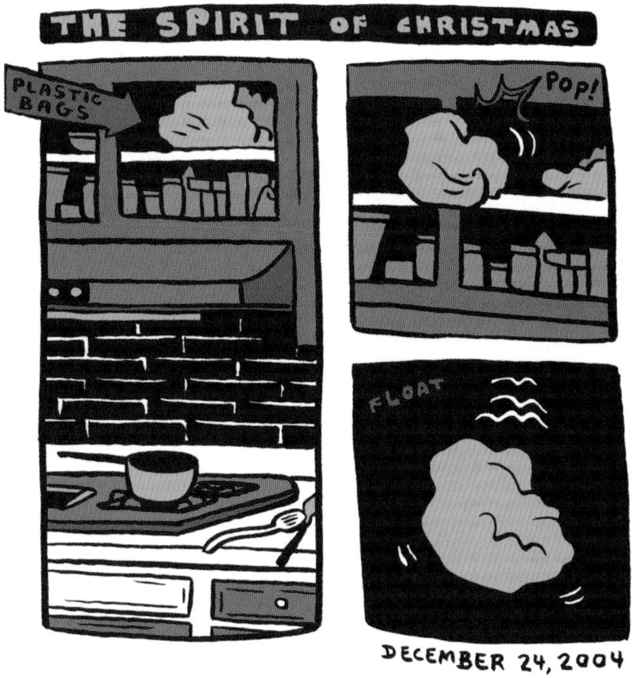
THE SPIRIT OF CHRISTMAS
PLASTIC BAGS
POP!
FLOAT
DECEMBER 24, 2004

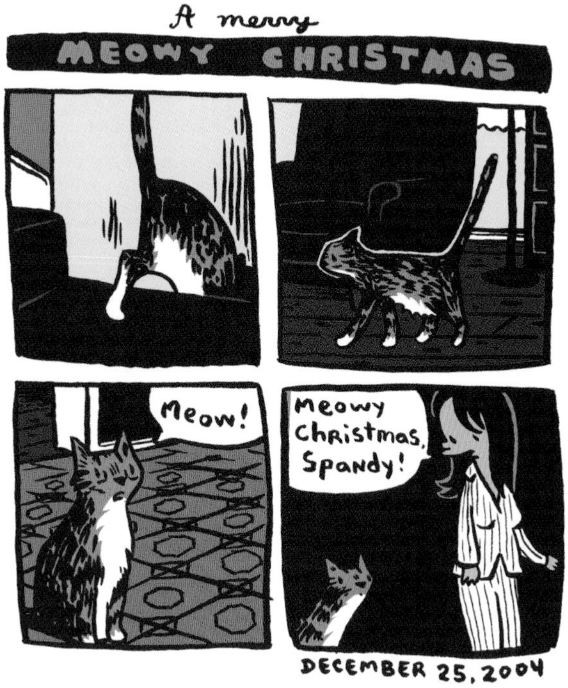
A merry
MEOWY CHRISTMAS
Meow!
Meowy Christmas, Spandy!
DECEMBER 25, 2004

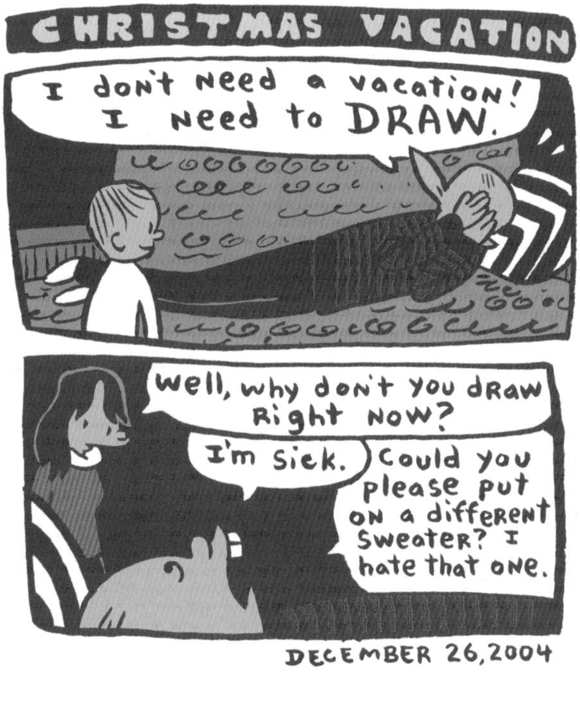
CHRISTMAS VACATION
I don't need a vacation! I need to DRAW.
Well, why don't you draw Right now?
I'm sick.
Could you please put on a different sweater? I hate that one.
DECEMBER 26, 2004

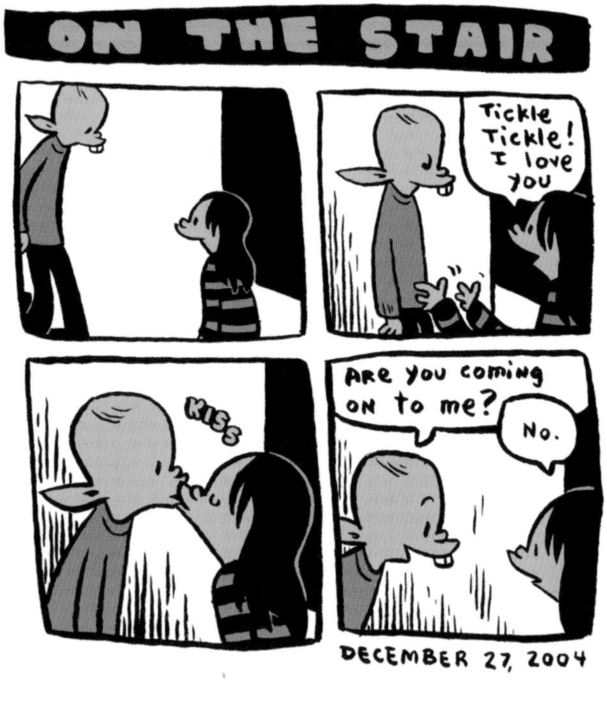
ON THE STAIR
Tickle Tickle! I love you
KISS
Are you coming on to me?
No.
DECEMBER 27, 2004

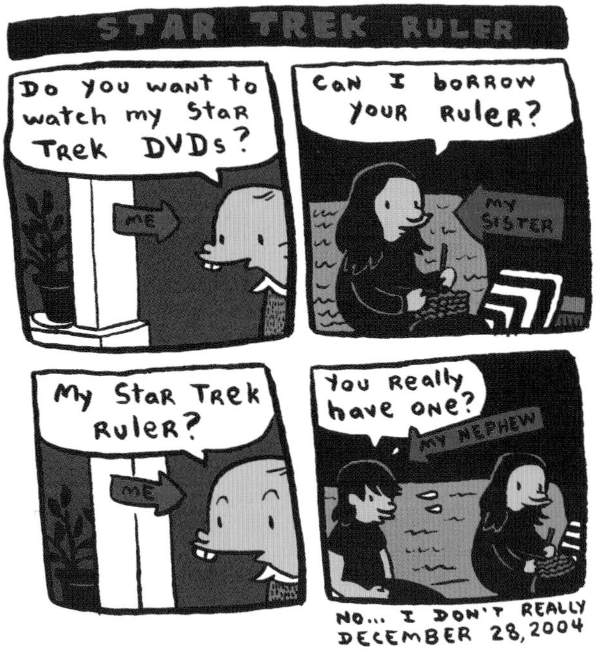
STAR TREK RULER
Do you want to watch my Star Trek DVDs?
ME
Can I borrow your ruler?
MY SISTER
My Star Trek ruler?
ME
You really have one?
MY NEPHEW
NO... I DON'T REALLY
DECEMBER 28, 2004

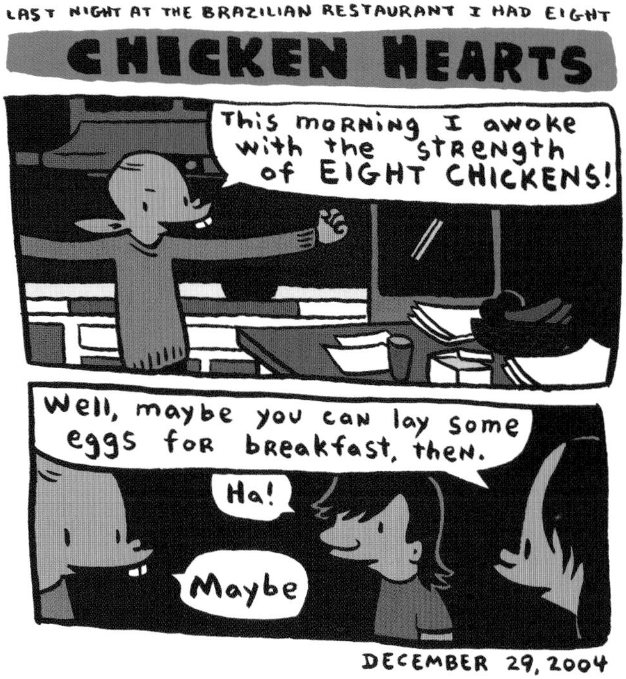
LAST NIGHT AT THE BRAZILIAN RESTAURANT I HAD EIGHT
CHICKEN HEARTS
This morning I awoke with the strength of EIGHT CHICKENS!
Well, maybe you can lay some eggs for breakfast, then.
Ha!
Maybe
DECEMBER 29, 2004

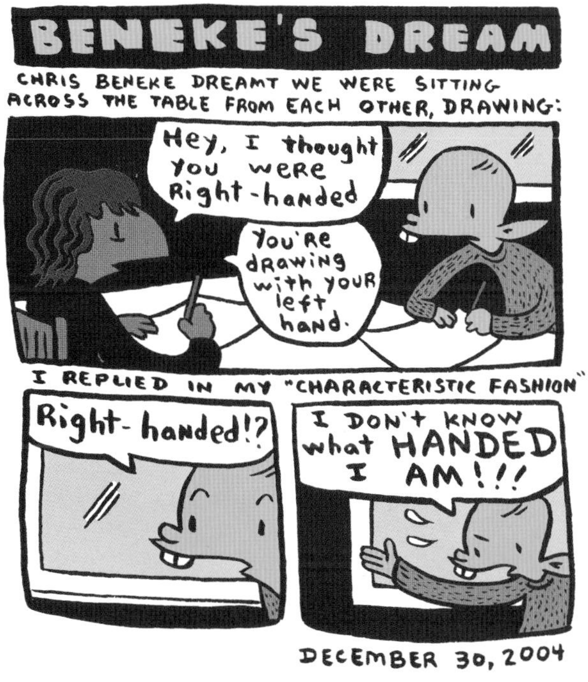
BENEKE'S DREAM
CHRIS BENEKE DREAMT WE WERE SITTING ACROSS THE TABLE FROM EACH OTHER, DRAWING:
Hey, I thought you were Right-handed
You're drawing with your left hand.
I REPLIED IN MY "CHARACTERISTIC FASHION"
Right-handed!?
I DON'T KNOW what HANDED I AM!!!
DECEMBER 30, 2004

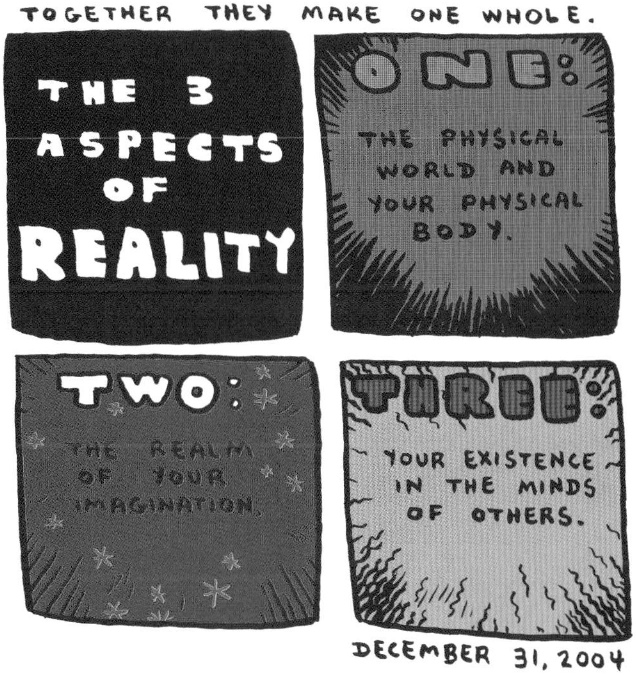
TOGETHER THEY MAKE ONE WHOLE.
THE 3 ASPECTS OF REALITY
ONE:
THE PHYSICAL WORLD AND YOUR PHYSICAL BODY.
TWO:
THE REALM OF YOUR IMAGINATION.
THREE:
YOUR EXISTENCE IN THE MINDS OF OTHERS.
DECEMBER 31, 2004

"HAPPY" NEW YEAR

Is it just me, or is everybody slightly depressed about the New Year?

bh

No, I think that's about Right

JANUARY 1, 2005

THE CARTOONIST'S WIFE

I think I've got this story figured out now, finally.

Have you decided what to name the characters?

No...

How about Spoony-E and Spandy-3?

That's good! I'll just write a spoon into the story.

JANUARY 2, 2005

THE SAME PERSON

ALTHOUGH I HAVE CHANGED MUCH OVER MY LIFETIME, TODAY I SUDDENLY SAW THE CONNECTEDNESS OF IT ALL.

!!?

I'm the same PERSON I was when I was a little kid!

Still drawing comics. I'm still ME.

JANUARY 3, 2005

SELF TAUGHT

zhuk

Eli is unwinding the tape.

That sounds VERY educational

Yeah, he's learning about stickiness and trouble-making.

JANUARY 4, 2005

OH, FRIENDSHIP

I HAVEN'T SEEN JOSH IN WEEKS.

O.K. Bye-bye Josh

CLICK

Whoops! I forgot to tell Josh that I've been bad-mouthing her to everyone

I already told her.

JANUARY 5, 2005

CAT PHOTOGRAPHY

good, GREAT!

FLASH

Gorgeous!

FLASH

NO, Spandy!

Stop closing your eyes!

FLASH

JANUARY 6, 2005

BUNNY-MONKEY

I WROTE A NEW JOKE TODAY, WHILE PUSHING ELI IN HIS STROLLER.

"What's the difference between a Bunny Monkey and a Honey Monkey?"

BUT WHEN I TOLD IT TO AMY, SHE DIDN'T LIKE IT.

Well, a Bunny-Monkey eats BananaCarrots...

...and a Honey-Monkey has sticky genitals!

ha ha!

What?!

JANUARY 7, 2005

LOTION

Will you put Eli to bed?

Well, then you have to draw today's strip.

O.K.

LATER

Did you finish?

No

Did you start?

I had to put lotion on my hands

JANUARY 8, 2005

LITTLE BLUE RECTANGLE

LATE AT NIGHT, ACROSS THE STREET, THROUGH THE WINDOWS, THROUGH THE TREES, I CAN SEE THE LITTLE BLUE RECTANGLE OF THE NEIGHBOR'S T.V.

JANUARY 9, 2005

SICK TOMATO

ELI STAYED HOME SICK FROM DAY CARE

tomatoes!

PEE WEE ON DVD

ha ha

LATER Eli laughed when Pee Wee put tomatoes on his salad.

He loves tomatoes

JANUARY 10, 2005

USEFUL SUPERSTITION

YOU CAN HELP PREVENT HOUSE FIRES BY PUTTING A PENNY ABOVE THE DOORWAYS IN YOUR HOME. (ESPECIALLY ON THE ENTRANCES.)

ELI'S HAIR GETS CRAZIER EVERY DAY.

PERHAPS IT'S ONE OF THE SIDE EFFECTS.

JANUARY 11, 2005

DADDY'S WOOD STOVE

No, honey. You can't make a fire in the wood stove. Only daddies can do that.

ba?

Someday, when you're older... and you make love to your wife...

hey, COME BACK! I'm not finished

JANUARY 12, 2005

BURNY FEELING

I LEFT MY SWIMSUIT AT KATE'S WEDDING LAST SUMMER SO I CAN'T GO IN THE POOL TODAY. INSTEAD I'M JUST STANDING BY THE SIDE.

The water on the floor feels like it's burning my toes!

Sorta itchy too

CORRECTION

YESTERDAY, I DREW THE GATE AROUND THE WOODSTOVE LIKE THIS:

BUT IT REALLY LOOKS MORE LIKE THIS:

JANUARY 13, 2005

THE CONDIMENT KID

Don't drink your ketchup

THE END

JANUARY 14, 2005

FASCINATING MAGAZINE

OVER AT ALAN & TRIXIE'S HOUSE

Are you listening? Stop Reading magazines

LATER

So, anyhow then...

James?

This is a fascinating magazine

JANUARY 15, 2005

LIME TIME

Oh! I accidentally put salt in the lime-ade.

It's kinda awful

Amy, aren't you going to taste it?

No

Oh come on

No! why would I even want to? You said it was awful.

Okay, but you're REALLY missing out!

JANUARY 16, 2005

HOT POT

Look out! Hot! Hot!!

well, maybe Not So hot.

Warm! Warm!

JANUARY 17, 2005

YESTERDAY, I WAS FURIOUS.

I DON'T KNOW WHAT MADE ME THINK I COULD FIND A PAIR OF SWIM SHORTS I LIKE.

they're all HUGE

TODAY, NOT FURIOUS AT ALL.

ELI'S IN DAY CARE, WHICH MEANS I'M WORKING HARD ON MY COMICS AND THAT'S ALL I'M THINKING ABOUT.

OCCASIONALLY I PAUSE FROM MY WORK TO NOTICE THAT I NEED TO SHAVE.

JANUARY 18, 2005

RADIATION X

I wonder if the x-rays will activate my latent powers

LATER

JANUARY 19, 2005

THIS YELLOW ROSE IS DYING

Guess how much money I've made So far this year!

One hundred dollars.

Today?

No, this year

Well, good for you.

thanks

JANUARY 20, 2005

DON'T FEAR THE DEVIL

LAST NIGHT (AT OUR ROCK SHOW)

So... lately my TV has started feeding-back.

Probably, it's the Devil

Oh, good... I thought it might be electrical

like "Oh, him? I've been dealing with him my whole life"

JANUARY 21, 2005

PUNCHING THE DEVIL

ow

How did I skin my knuckles in my sleep?

LATER Maybe I skinned my knuckle while we were making love?

No

JANUARY 22, 2005

TRY NEW FOODS

BURDOCK ROOT

Cut it into matchstick size strips...

CHOP

The IROQUOIS liked it, and so do the Japanese. Hmm... sweet & bitter.

CRUNCH

RAW

Nice

LATER It's fun to try new foods but that aftertaste is hell! My throat has been burning for over an hour.

"Budrock Burdock" would be a good Name for a villain

JANUARY 23, 2005

MY WINTER COSTUME

I love this!

!!

It's so FUNNY to make eye contact with people who can't see my face.

SMILING

JANUARY 24, 2005

JANUARY 25, 2005

JANUARY 26, 2005

JANUARY 27, 2005

JANUARY 28, 2005

CORRECTIONS: THE BURDOCK I ATE THE
OTHER DAY WAS NOT BURDOCK.

JAR JAR CUP

Meesa tickle you!

Ha ha ha ha ha!

NAP TIME

ARRR!

LATER If you want Eli to fall asleep, all you have to do is hold him tight and surf the internet for an hour.

z

JANUARY 29, 2005

FULL FROM AMY'S BIRTHDAY DINNER &
KNOCKED OUT

Goodnight honey

Can't

draw comic strip

JANUARY 30, 2005

TELEVISION ENERGY

She has AWFUL hair.

Amy?

I don't know.

It's a hair ad but her hair is AWFUL!

I just watch T.V. for entertainment.

I don't get all excited

Oh

JANUARY 31, 2005

DON'T EAT AMY'S FLOWERS

where is it?

hmm

It's gotta be somewhere!

Spandy, I heard you PUKING, so where is it?

Where's the puke?

FEBRUARY 1, 2005

OH, NONE OF 'EM ARE

Oh, before you go... do you know where the word "computer" came from?

No, where?

The first ones were made from cum & pewter!

Is that one of your home made jokes?

Yeah!

It's not one of your better ones.

FEBRUARY 2, 2005

OLD MACDONALD HAD AN ARGUMENT:

♪...with a woof woof here and a—

Wait, Stop!

That's not how "Old MacDonald" goes.

Yes it is.

Not with the repeating all the animals

It's fun that way.

But you're adding an extra beat to each measure.

It's just WRONG!

FEBRUARY 3, 2005

WARM GENTLE THROB

WARM GENTLE THROB

ow

LATER

How was your day with Eli?

My earlobe has a fever.

FEBRUARY 4, 2005

THE PAIN OF THE CRIPPLED AVENGER

LAST NIGHT But if I stay up for the midnight Kung-Fu I'll be miserable tomorrow.

But what about my family? They don't want to see me like that.

TODAY

oh settle down

FU CK YOU!

COFFEE SPLASH

FEBRUARY 5, 2005

AXIS MUNDI

THE SPIRE OF THE CHURCH CAST A SHADOW IN THE GLOW OF BURLINGTON AND DIVIDED THE SKY INTO LIGHT & DARK.

FEBRUARY 6, 2005

SOCKS & FEELINGS

I'm talking to Daddy about my thoughts & feelings

eh?

No thoughts & feelings NOT socks & feelings.

FEBRUARY 7, 2005

LEMONS & ICE

Eesh!

tINKLE

Isn't that too cold?

Doesn't it hurt?

Eli?

Lemons in his mouth and his hand soaking in ice... he CAN'T be happy.

Yet he is

FEBRUARY 8, 2005

I LUV U

Hi, this is James... IS Amy there?

WAITING TO BE CONNECTED...

I love you!

AMY IS SICK OF ME ALWAYS CALLING HER AT WORK.

FEBRUARY 9, 2005

THE ART OF DRAWING

I'm going to draw my strip now.

Woo!

WOOSH

Just kidding

FEBRUARY 10, 2005

AFTER SIX MONTHS, FINALLY! ELI LEARNED HOW TO MAKE THE HARMONICA WORK:

Wheeze wheeze tweet

AND PRACTICED SAYING HIS NEW CATCH PHRASE IN THE WONDERFULLY ELASTIC WAY HE DOES.

Oh, WOWW!

Oh, WOW!

I SAW A CLOUD THAT I LIKED ESPECIALLY WELL,

AND WITH A QUAVERING VOICE ANNOUNCED:

We're so lucky to live on such a beautiful planet

FEBRUARY 11, 2005

SICK ALL DAY

SNAP

I guess Daddy's feeling better if he's dancing again!

Woo!

FEBRUARY 12, 2005

POSITIVELY

Oooh! It's so fluffy!

So light!

SHOOF

This doesn't hurt my back at all.

I will never be unhappy again.

FEBRUARY 13, 2005

NO PROBLEM

I accidentally vowed to never be unhappy again.

I know

It's rather alarming.

Hey!

FEBRUARY 14, 2005

LIST OF WORDS

Mommy & I made a list of all the words you can say, Eli. There's bottle*, there ya go, hat, this, that, DUCK, meow, woof, SNOW**, hot, No, Yeah Yeah Yeah, More ***, hi, hello, bye, Eli ****, uh-oh, DVD and one-two-three *****!

Ha ha ha!

* PRONOUNCE WITH NO "T" SOUND ** PRONOUNCED WITH A SILENT "S" *** IN SIGN LANGUAGE **** PRONOUNCED "IYAH" ***** BOTH PRONOUNCED "DEE DEE DOO"

Wait, there's MORE: Rarr! Hmm? VRoom! ball, Ba-ba, Elmo, Tick-tock, bzz, fish, Shh, Oh wow, Woo!

Woo!

FEBRUARY 15, 2005

A SNOWY SNACK

I PUT OUT A BOWL TO CATCH SNOW

BUT I WAITED TOO LONG TO RETRIEVE IT

The snow turned to rain and brown stuff dripped off the tree. It's ruined.

Sorry!

FEBRUARY 16, 2005

SSSSASHAAAA!

RING

RING

RING

LET'S GET DRUNK

Okay!

FEBRUARY 17, 2005

SOUND & FURY

What a terrible print job! These comics must be like only 300 Dpi!

I have no idea what you're talking about.

Well, look, it's hardly got any hit points.
?

It's like the work of a 2nd level Magic-User!
Ha!

FEBRUARY 18, 2005

CRUMBLY CASCADE

ERASER CRUMBLIES FROM MY DRAWING TABLE,

CASCADE DOWN THE STAIRS,

AND ARE NEARLY IMPOSSIBLE TO CLEAN OFF THE CARPET WHEN COMPANY'S COMING OVER.

SCRUF SCRUF

FEBRUARY 19, 2005

CUTE OBSESSIONS

ELI WENT TO SLEEP HOLDING HIS BALLOON

FEBRURYY 20, 2005

SHIRT OF THE DAY

ELI'S FACE STARTED TO BREAK OUT.

THAT NIGHT I HAD DREAMS THAT HE WAS DEFORMED.

WE WOKE UP TO A BEAUTIFUL FLUFFY SNOW.

I DRESSED HIM IN THE SHIRT HE WORE IN MY DREAM, I THINK.

RUARY 21, 2005

LET IT GO

"Well, they were fucking up my T.V. show."

"The writers wanted to put ELVIS in it."

"Anyhow, I think I might've gotten them fired."

"So I made a power play to take it over myself, but I think that backfired."

FEBRUARY 22, 2005

EVERYONE WAS AFRAID TO TALK TO HIM ABOUT IT, BUT NOT ME!

FORGET ME NOT

"Dad, you should get tested for Alzheimer's"

"They have medecine for that now."

"Oh, Really? They can do that? My goodness."

"Oh, wow"

"GREAT!"

"I'll tell Mom you said okay!"

FEBRUARY 23, 2005

TRAVEL INK

"ARR!"

"It can't be opened!"

"it's inked shut"

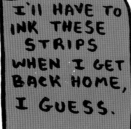

I'LL HAVE TO INK THESE STRIPS WHEN I GET BACK HOME, I GUESS.

FEB 24, 2005

GRANDMA'S COUCH *

"Snif Snif"

"It still smells like Eli's vomit."

* AMY'S MOM'S

FEBRUARY 25, 2005

LOVE TOUGH

No, the clock is NOT Right. I was hoping tough love would work, but I guess I'll just have to set it for you.

Someone on the Comics Journal message board today tried to use tough love on me, too.

And it didn't work. Did it? You're Resistant to "tough love"

FEBRUARY 26, 2005

VOW OF HAPPINESS

Yeah, so... I took a Vow of Happiness.

Really?

Amy says I'm always a miserable jerk and have been for the last twenty years!

All this time I thought I was happy!

Imagine my SURPRISE!

"Imagine my SURPRISE". So... how does this vow work?

If I notice I'm getting unhappy, I just Remind myself to be happy

How did you come to take a vow like that?

I was shoveling snow and it was so fluffy I said I'd NEVER be unhappy again.

FEBRUARY 27, 2005

HANGING FROM THE END OF THE TWIG WAS AN
UNUSUAL ICICLE

FEBRUARY 28, 2005

SEE YA LATER

Drain the tub NOW.

FUCK!

SHLURP

Eli's washcloth got sucked Right down the drain!

It doesn't seem to matter though

You scared Eli when you yelled

MARCH 1, 2005

KA-CHUNK

LAST NIGHT I PUT UP ROCK POSTERS IN THE SNOW.

TODAY, I WONDER IF THEY'VE ALL BEEN TORN DOWN OR POSTERED OVER ALREADY?

BUT IT ALMOST DOESN'T MATTER 'CAUSE I THOROUGHLY ENJOYED HANGING THEM.

MARCH 2, 2005

HIT THE GOLDEN CEILING

Um... can I get paid now?

SURE

And here's the band's TAB for the bar.

What!?

The other guys didn't PAY before they left?!!? How much does this all come to?!?

Let's see... eight dollars!

Oh.

No problem, then.

AT ONE-HALF

MARCH 3, 2005

TOE NULL

I really really need to cut my toenails

Well, why don't you?

I CAN'T

I've always got SOCKS ON.

MARCH 4, 2005

20 SECONDS IN THE MICROWAVE

BEEP

Wow! 20 seconds goes by FAST!

I know! Just think of all the 20 seconds we've wasted in life!

MARCH 5, 2005

STROLLER

WE CAN'T MAKE IT HOME IN THIS

"This thing is hard to push"

"It's not broken. Oh... yeah it is."

SO WE JUST CHUCKED IT IN SOME RANDOM DUMPSTER

CLUNK

HAPPENED YESTERDAY, DRAWN TODAY

MARCH 6, 2005

G J & S & T

"Grape juice & seltzer?"

"Yeah!"

"And another piece of toast!"

"IN YOUR DRINK?"

"No!"

"too late"

"Wha-?!"

"You're funny."

MARCH 7, 2005

STROLLER AND SLED

IT'S LATE LAST NIGHT BUT ELI REALLY REALLY WANTS TO TRY HIS NEW STROLLER, SO WE DO. THE NEW STROLLER SUCKS, PLUS IT RAINS.

I MANAGE TO PLACATE MY ANGER BY WATCHING RAINDROPS SPLASH AND THINKING ABOUT HOW MUCH MY COLD HANDS HURT.

NOW IT'S TODAY. A LAYER OF ICE UNDER THE FRESH SNOW MAKES IT EASY TO PULL THE SLED OVER STREET AND SIDEWALK.

"Jingle bells Jingle bells"

MARCH 8, 2005

MORNING ADVENTURES

"Give me your hand"

"That's my penis"

LATER

"There it is again"

"Yes, but now it's not hard."

MARCH 9, 2005

MUSIC LESSONS

HiSS!

tweet?

I don't think kitty WANTS to play harmonica

SSSS - ffoo - SSSS - ffoo*

*SUCK - BLOW - SUCK - BLOW   MARCH 10, 2005

SQUIRT

we could plant the grapefruit seeds.

would that really work?

Sure... it wouldn't grow fruit but it would grow

What if the seeds aren't fertilized?

You can fertilize them.

Should I go jerk off on the grapefruit?

MARCH 11, 2005

STRIPS THAT SUCKED

JANUARY 3RD, 2005

I'm still ME.

NOVEMBER 16, 2004

SEPTEMBER 16, 2004

Whoo!

JULY 4, 2004

MARCH 12, 2005

MY WINE JOURNAL

Got to clear my mind... what does it smell like?

Manure & bleach with a hint of leather...

No... it's not BLEACH, that's too extreme.

It's magic marker and some kind of detergent! No... not detergent, ... CONDITIONER!

MARCH 13, 2005

COMPETING SUNBEAMS

I HAVE NOT DRAWN ANY OF MY MELTDOWNS, FREAKOUTS, OR TANTRUMS IN A WHILE. I JUST DON'T FEEL LIKE DRAWING THEM. USUALLY SOME OTHER LITTLE THING FROM THE DAY ENDS UP STRIKING ME AS BEING MORE IMPORTANT.

JUST FINISHED DOING TAXES →

Ooh. Competing Sunbeams!

MARCH 14, 2005

INTERESTING DISCOVERY

Something smells like pot.

It's this grapefruit!

SNIF

hey, you're Right

NAME CHANGE

You know how you say my sketchbook diaries are neither truly sketchbooks NOR diaries?

Should I call them "portable drawing book autobiographical comic strips"?

IS THAT better?

MARCH 15, 2005

BRAIN WAVES

It smells like glacier ice and tree bark.

WINE

LATER

I wonder if Jason Cooley is dead?

MARCH 16, 2005

PLAY TIME

Cough

I suppose if I REALLY needed to know if Jason was alive or dead, I could read his "blog."

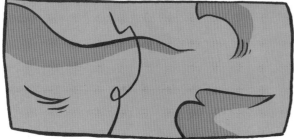

COUGH! COUGH! COUGH!

MARCH 17, 2005

CRACKERS

DOWN THE STEPS!   MARCH 18, 2005

HIS MAJESTY

MARCH 19, 2005

ELI FALLS DOWN

MARCH 20, 2005

ACTING OUT MY HUMAN FEELINGS

MARCH 21, 2005

BATTLE EMPATHY

Eli!

Ow! Daddy's mouth!

Oh

PAT PAT

MARCH 22, 2005

WHO'S THE RETARD, NOW?

They know who the * Rapist & murderer is.

Who?

Our Neighbor, Wisdom. **

The guy who thought I was RETARDED!?

* ALLEGED
** NOT HIS REAL NAME

MARCH 23, 2005

ROCK TIME

Don't let me forget to go to my Rock show tonight

Alright. What time do you have to be there?

I don't even know!

MARCH 24, 2005

REPEATING WHAT THE GIRL SAID

That was a great show! You made me wet!

and then she said "one day Eli will make a tremendous lover".

Ha!

MARCH 25, 2005

BUNNY POX

ELI MET THE EASTER BUNNY

Hi!

THEN

Oh... are you getting a cold sore?

WE WENT TO GRANDMA & GRANPA'S

Wake up. The CD'S starting over

IT LOOKS LIKE GRANPA MIGHT BE GETTING A COLD SORE TOO.

Aye ya ya!
Aye bla bla

MARCH 26, 2005

EASTER HAPPY

The key to happiness...

...might be matching shirt & underwear.
GREEN

MUCH EARLIER

Look, Eli! Grandma & Grandpa!
blink blink

MARCH 27, 2005

IN BED, AT NIGHT, IN THE DARK, WITH MY EYES CLOSED...

WHEN I COUGH I SEE "SPARKS."

COUGH COUGH

AND I LIKE IT.

COUGH

MARCH 28, 2005

THE SOFTEST DOZEN

DOZENS OF THE SOFTEST, SWEETEST KISSES...

meh

STILL ARE NOT ENOUGH.

ba ba?
Grunt

Eli, what are you doing to Daddy's head?
BOUNCE BOUNCE
GAH!

MARCH 29, 2005

EYES OF THE SNOWMAN

SNOWMAN

Eyes!

Yup, his eyes fell out again

There

MARCH 30, 2005

LITTLE ELI NAPPING IN HIS CRIB, UNAWARE THAT HACKERS HAVE DOWNED HIS DADDY'S WEBSITE.

MARCH 31, 2005

ALMOND BUTTER

TOMORROW I FLY TO HOUSTON WITH MY BAND.

IF THE PLANE CRASHES, TODAY MIGHT BE THE LAST DAY OF MY LIFE.

AMY'S AT WORK. ELI'S IN DAYCARE.

I'M SPENDING THE LAST DAY OF MY LIFE FEELING WEIRD.

APRIL 1, 2005

LONE STAR STATE

Man, they got stars on everything here

Shut up

Deep in the heart Of Texas!

CLAP CLAP CLAP CLAP

♪ THAT SONG

APRIL 2, 2005

HALF WAY HOME

FIELD OF BLUE LIGHTS

TURBULANCE DURING TAKE OFF

THIS COMIC STRIP IS PROBABLY ONE OF THE SHITTIEST OF ALL TIME. I HAVE RISEN ABOVE PEDESTRIAN NOTIONS OF QUALITY. I AM A SOARING FLYING GOD.

APRIL 3, 2005

WEEKEND SUMMARY

GOT UP WICKED EARLY, THEN FLEW TO TEXAS, DID A COMIC BOOK SIGNING, PLAYED A ROCK SHOW, WENT TO BED, GOT UP, PLAYED A ROCK SHOW, FLEW BACK HOME & GOT IN BED.

I feel very strange, I think

APRIL 4, 2005

LOST THE VOICE

No! Don't step on the Raspberry plant!

what are you so cranky about?

I'm not the one who stepped on the raspberry plant!

I didn't step on it

Yes you did!

APRIL 5, 2005

SMALL PRINT

maybe we should use that baby seat for our flight to D.C.

It's in the trash

You're not supposed to get 'em that way?

"Warranty void if found by a dumpster"

APRIL 6, 2005

UPLOADER

I SPENT 2 ½ HOURS RE-UPLOADING ALL THE AMERICAN ELF STRIPS SINCE MAY 2002 ONTO THE NEW SERVER.

This is boring.

It's a little bit fun, I guess

cuddly

boring
But almost done

APRIL 7, 2005

SPRING ONLINE

THE BIRDS ARE BACK IN THE BATHROOM CEILING.

tweet tweet

BRIGHT SUNSHINE'S STREAMING IN THE WINDOWS.

MY DIARY IS BACK ONLINE!

AMERICAN ELF .COM

APRIL 8, 2005

I HEARD DUCKS...

Quack Quack

THEIR QUACKING SOUNDED A LITTLE LIKE THEY WERE PLAYING GAMEBOY

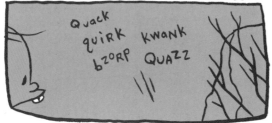
Quack quirk kwank bzorp QUAZZ

APRIL 9, 2005

LOVERS

Come on, let's get it over with!
Woo!
we're going to get it over with!!!

APRIL 10, 2005

CAT SAFETY

You can come out of the closet today, Spandy.

Eli's in day care.

APRIL 11, 2005

A STORY ABOUT DINNER

what are we going to have for dinner?

hmm...

I don't know!

Yum!

(LAST NIGHT)

APRIL 12, 2005

TOO BUSY

Do you want to come spend time with Me & Eli?

James?

Uh, NO thanks!

Just kidding!

APRIL 13, 2005

THE SPOUSE'S MOUTH

Give me a kiss!

with my PENIS?

No, with your kisser.

SMACK

IN THE RED ROOM, APPROXIMATELY 4:30 PM

APRIL 14, 2005

SCRATCHES

It didn't leave a mark... Good

But if I bump the wall __every__ time I carry laundry down the stairs that can't be good.

APRIL FIFTEEN 2005

OUR LONG HISTORY

Last night, when you were telling those guys all the old stories about what a bad boyfriend I used to be, it made me really sad.

but those are some of my favorite stories!

Really? Well.... then are you disappointed that I'm not so bad anymore?

No... I still have a LOT of work to do ON you.

APRIL 16, 2005

WOMEN GLITTER

I've been thinking about this for a while...

Do you think I could get rich if I made a woman's lotion with all these properties? scented, moisturizing, anti-wrinkle, acne-treatment, sunscreen, self-tanning, hair growth inhibiting, bug repellant, antibacterial, birth control ... and Glitter!

Did I miss anything?

Would that meet all of a woman's needs?

hmm

Put it in a vibrating bottle?

APRIL 17, 2005

I SENT INSTRUCTIONS TO TOM DEVLIN TO RESCUE ALL THE ARTWORK FROM MY HARDDRIVE IF ME & MY FAMILY DIE IN A PLANE CRASH. I'M NOT WORRIED BUT I

WANNA BE PREPARED

LAST NIGHT I MADE A LIST OF EVERYTHING WE NEED TO DO BEFORE OUR TRIP TO D.C.

AND THEN I LEFT IT WHERE WE MIGHT REMEMBER TO SEE IT.

TODAY I HAVEN'T LOOKED AT THE LIST BUT I THINK I'M REMEMBERING EVERYTHING.

My sleves look a little too short.

APRIL 18, 2005

WHAT'S UP WITH THOSE SUNGLASSES?

What do you want to do in D.C.?

Ooh... maybe we could get one of those twelve dollar CORN DOGS!

Good idea

APRIL 19, 2005

ANIMAL FACTS AT THE ZOO

blink blink

I had no idea chickens had such large genitals!
They do?

WASHINGTON, D.C.   APRIL 20, 2005

VACATION IS FUN

It's fun to wake up in the morning!
Yay!

It's fun to say hi to everyone who boards the metro!
Hi!

thereyago!
PAT PAT
I don't think they want to sit on daddy's lap

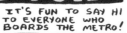
It's fun to run up and down the halls in Chris & Kate's building, screaming!
WOOO!

APRIL 21, 2005
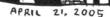

THE RASPBERRY CHRONICLES

Don't step on the Raspberry plant!!!!

I didn't

Yeah, but LAST time you did!

APRIL 22, 2005

FEELING THE BEAR'S HEAD

There's something hard inside the bear's head.

It's his BRAIN, of course

APRIL 23, 2005

LATER... UPON FURTHER REFLECTION I DECIDE IT'S MORE LIKELY GOTTA BE HIS SKULL.

SAMURAI BALLOON DANCING

LISTENING TO THE BAND "COLLIDER"

APRIL 24, 2005

LITTLE BIRD

Should we clip his wings?

& OTHER CHOICES:

IT'S TIME TO START WORK ON A NEW BOOK. I'M NOT SURE WHICH IDEA TO USE OR WHAT.

A squirrel in the rain...

Monsters on a mountain...

APRIL 25, 2005

TRULY BEING ALIVE

You're just a sub-par Har Mar Superstar ♫

NAG!

K-ONK

Aah!

Aah! Aah! Aah!

APRIL 26, 2005

SQUIRRELLY GRAY

ON THE COMPUTER I TYPED ALL THE DAY, COMPOSING VERSE FOR MY BOOK "SQUIRRELLY GRAY."

Here I go!

ALMOST FINISHED, I DECIDED TO SWITCH A COMMA FOR PERIOD, DUMB SILLY BITCH!

It crashed!

WIRP

I LOST ALL THE TEXT AND BECAME QUITE UPSET, BUT I GATHERED MY WITS TO THINK WHAT TO DO NEXT.

What do I do?

I SEARCHED THE COMPUTER FOR INVISIBLE FILES, AND FOUND THE TEXT GARBLED, WHICH I THEN RECOMPILED.

Easy as pie!

TYPE TYPE

APRIL 27, 2005

ANECTDOTALLY
HOIST BY MY OWN PETARD

So, yesterday I was typing this story but then the computer crashed and I lost everything, but then I—

—I know

I read your strip online.

Oh

huh.

APRIL 28, 2005

I TAKE THE FOLDER OF TINY PAINTINGS FROM MY BOOKSHELF.

SHE'S TRYING TO DECIDE WHICH ONE TO BUY FOR HER BROTHER.

HER HANDS ARE SHAKING. SHE'S NERVOUS.

I'M NOT SURE HOW TO PUT HER MORE AT EASE.

Perhaps I should look away.

APRIL 29, 2005

NEW THING

This is my new story.

You didn't capitalize your last name.

yeah

Is that your new "thing"?

No!

APRIL 30, 2005

BACKUP PLAN

I want to play DOOM 3.

But I have to wait until Eli goes to bed to do that. And that's when I was hoping to have sex with Amy.

Amy... do you think I can have sex with you AND play DOOM 3?

Not very likely

Well... one or the other I guess.

MAY 1, 2005

FIVE MONSTERS FOR MONDAY

MAY 2, 2005

TRAGEDY

Oh.

SCOOT SCOOT

Three pieces of rice on my plate spelled out the letter H...

But then I killed it.

MAY 3, 2005

MY PROOFREADER

well... it's a good story...

But your rhymes and cadence are all messed up.

This rough draft has a lot more life to it.

How long have you been working on this?

Like... ten years.

Sort of.

Well... work a little longer.

MAY 4, 2005

INVISIBLE BEE

Bee! Bee!

There's a bee? Where?

Bee

Aah! Bee!

MAY 5, 2005

SOME WOMAN IN TOWN

You don't remember me, do you?

Well... I recognize you.

"ISOTOPIC SPIN" BY CLARK RUSSELL IN BACKGROUND

MAY 6, 2005

SPINNING

Wow! So she saved some guy's life today?

Yup! What did you do today?

Nothin', I guess.

You did an interview with SPIN magazine today.

oh yeah!

That's something

MAY 7, 2005

ROMANCE OF LIFE

Mother's day is the new Valentine's

GETTING OLDER

Ow!

I guess my finger isn't as young as it used to be.

MAY 8, 2005

FEELING GREAT

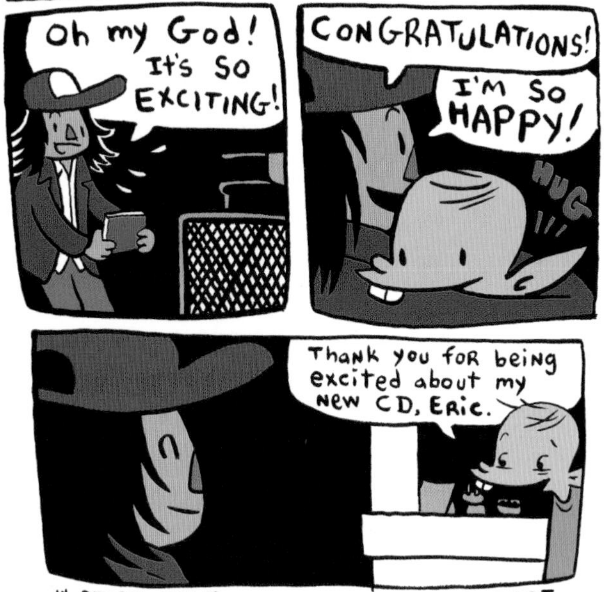
Oh my God! It's so EXCITING!
CONGRATULATIONS!
I'm so HAPPY!
HUG
Thank you for being excited about my new CD, Eric.

IN STORES MAY 10

MAY 9, 2005

OUR MOST BELOVED

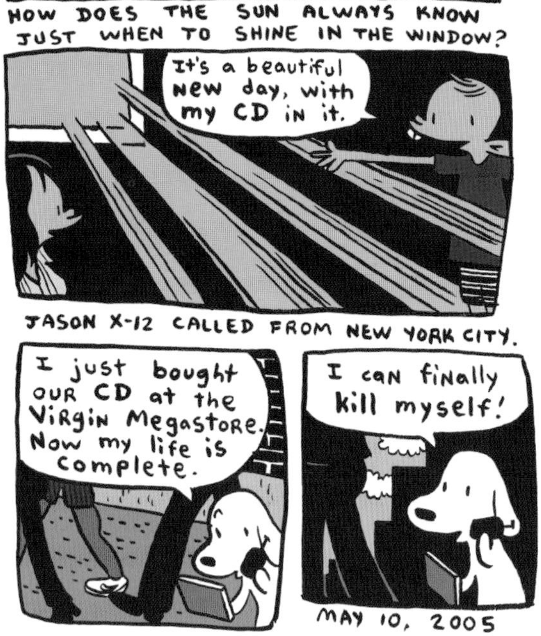
HOW DOES THE SUN ALWAYS KNOW JUST WHEN TO SHINE IN THE WINDOW?
It's a beautiful new day, with my CD in it.
JASON X-12 CALLED FROM NEW YORK CITY.
I just bought our CD at the Virgin Megastore. Now my life is complete.
I can finally kill myself!

MAY 10, 2005

PLEATHER ERROR

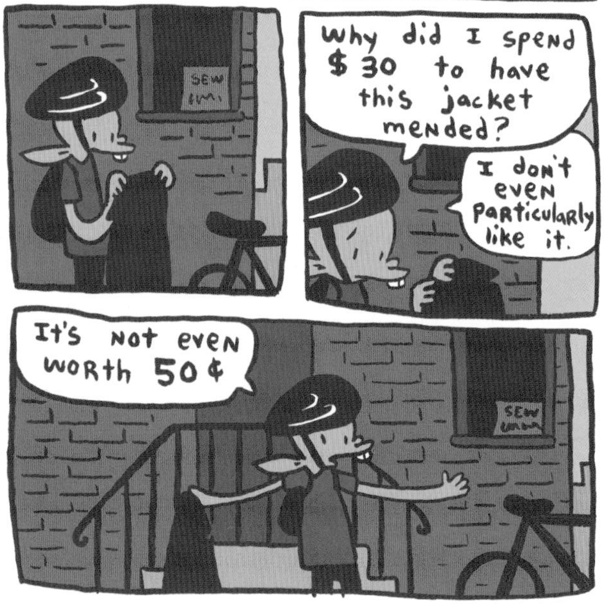
SEW
Why did I spend $30 to have this jacket mended?
I don't even particularly like it.
It's not even worth 50¢
SEW

MAY 11, 2005

LUCKY BOYS

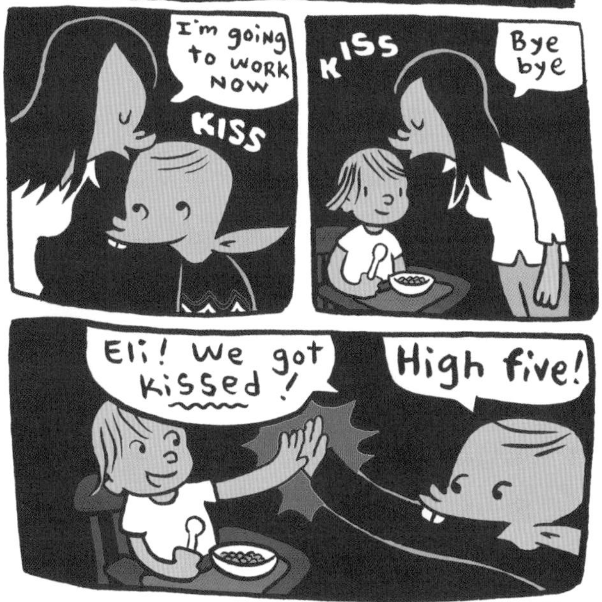
I'm going to work now
KISS
KISS
Bye bye
Eli! We got kissed!
High five!

MAY 12, 2005

PERFECTION

PEOPLE KEEP POINTING OUT ERRORS IN THE CREDITS ON MY C.D.

Another one!?

I NEGLECTED TO CREDIT TARQUIN.

He plays bass on almost every song!

I was BEST MAN at your wedding!

I CREDITED TOM LAWSON AS ONE OF THE MUSICIANS.

Tom doesn't play on ANY of these songs

I MISCREDITED PISTOL. HE CO-PRODUCED "TALK TO THE WOOKY" BUT I CREDITED HIM WITH CO-PRODUCING "OZZY & I"

ARRRRg

MAY 13, 2005

PERSPECTIVE

CAUGHT A GLIMPSE IN A MIRROR AT CITY MARKET

Eek!

I didn't know my hair looked that bad!

BRUSH BRUSH

I'll just get a haircut. SOON

MAY 14, 2005

DREAMING IN RHYME

I've been dreaming in rhyme.

That's a sign of insanity, isn't it?

I think it's because I'm working on a children's book

MAY 14, 2005

BATH TUB TIME

Do you want to tell daddy what happened?

Poo Poo

You went poo poo in the tub?

MAY 15, 2005

ELI'S COLD SORE MAP

A RECORD OF THEIR PLACEMENT ON HIS FACE DURING A RAPID BREAKOUT ON THIS DATE.

MAY 16, 2005

WAKE UP FROM YESTERDAY

Eli's face is almost all cleared up already.

either Acyclovir is a miracle drug or I imagined the whole thing

LATER
It cleared Right up!
He's a miracle baby!

MAY 17, 2005

PRIVATE TUTOR

I haven't tutored in a while.

You haven't tootered?

LATER
I suppose it doesn't matter as long as he's still pooping.
ha!

MAY 18, 2005

GET READY

Get Bikini Ready

what?
Oh, that magazine says "Get Bikini Ready"

I'm always bikini Ready!

MAY 19, 2005

WHEEE!

I MEET UP WITH TOM ON THE BUS TO WHITE RIVER JUNCTION VERMONT

Tom! James.

God, I love the giant windows on buses

wouldn't it be awesome if airplanes had windows like this?

MAY 20, 2005

REVENGE OF THE SITH

Oh No! I forgot Jar Jar!

We've got to stop back at my house to pick up my Jar Jar Binks cup!!

LATER... AT THE END OF THE MOVIE:

Meesa sad

FOOM

MAY 21, 2005

TICK TOCK SCRITCH

The clock is ticking, into the night.

With every passing second it becomes more difficult to start drawing this strip.

TICK TOCK TICK

TOCK

JUST BEGIN & FINISH IT QUICKLY, PLEASE.

SCRITCH SCRITCH

MAY 22, 2005

BABY FACE

Oh no!

His face is breaking out again!

Actually...

...that's just Magic Marker.

MAY 23, 2005

FLASH

I sent Spin Magazine an awesome photo of me & Eli making monster faces.

It was to accompany an interview with me about my book SUPERF*CKERS.

FLASH

But they say they don't think it's a good idea to have a picture of a baby on the same page as SuperF*ckers

He's not a baby. He's almost two!

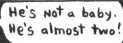

MAY 24, 2005

MIRACLE DONUT

The miracle donut is still there.

what in the world are you talking about?

MAY 25, 2005

JAMES KOCHALKA SUPERSTAR GETS A HAIRCUT

Aah... RUB FONDLE

I wonder if he's giving me an especially awesome head massage because he knows I'm a SUPERSTAR?

MAY 25, 2005

HAPPY BIRTHDAY TO ME

Happy Birthday to me ♫

Happy Birthday to me! I've got a New haircut... I'm so damn sexy! ♫

MAY 26, 2005

ROCK SHOW

BETWEEN SONGS I DRINK WATER. MAYBE FOUR OR FIVE PINTS.

THEN I PEE ALL NIGHT.

USHER

I'm so honored that Pete asked me to be best man at his wedding tomorrow.

You're Not best man.

well... fourth best.

what ever

DRAWN IN CONNECTICUT   MAY 27, 2005

NUMB THUMB   PAUL YATES

My thumb is numb. I wonder if I slept on it wrong?

If I spilled a glass of water on you would I make it into today's strip?

No!

CATHOLIC WEDDING   THE END

What's that stain?

Oh, when the PRIEST adjusted my flower I think he cummed on me.

My thumb is still numb?

Is this the beginning of the end of my drawing career

MAY 28, 2005

MORE HIGHLIGHTS FROM THE WEDDING
OF PETER KATIS AND ANN RISEN

LUCKY BONUS

Pete! Tarquin! I just saw your dad naked.

Yeah? Join the club.

High five!

DEMONS IN CHURCH

My skin is burning.

GLARF!

GAK!

HAPPENED MAY 28, but DRAWN MAY 29, 2005

SHE'S CALLING ME

RING

RING RING

It's the telephone!

RING

Hello, telephone!

MAY 30, 2005

THE GRAND STRUGGLE OF LIFE

INDOORS AND OUTDOORS...

It's one of the vines from outside.

I knew I shouldn't let them grow up the side of the house.

YANK

AND WHERE THE TWO HALVES OF HOUSE MEET TOGETHER:

Nooo!

DRIP

LATER

The boombox doesn't work anymore.

SKREECH

MAY 31, 2005

LEAKY ROOF HOLE

There's a tiny little hole under there

I'll take you to buy some sealer.

It sounds easy.

If this actually fixes your problem it will be AMAZING.

DRAWN 3 BEERS DRUNK,   JUNE 1, 2005

TRADE SECRETS

THERE was a big disaster this morning...

...but it all sorted itself out.

Sigh

What happened?

Oh nothing. Jeff thought his publishing company was going to go bankrupt.

JUNE 2, 2005

DANDELION BOYS

I've got so many little things I don't have time to do.

I've got a couple contracts and I don't even have time to sign them!

LATER

One...two...THREE!

TOSS

JUNE 3, 2005

TOENAIL CLIP CLAP

Look, Amy! I clipped my toenails

Yes, I could hear you.

Clip! Clip! CLIP!

CLAP CLAP CLAP

JUNE 4, 2005

FINE SPRAY ON A HOT DAY

Look, Eli

Ow!

Ssss

Ow!

Ow?

It's just water.

Ssss

I think he means it's cold.

Eek!

Ssss

JUNE 5, 2005

MY AMAZING MINISKIRT ADVENTURE

EARLIER

ISN'T that an amazing STORY?

hmph

ERIC... Amy isn't impressed with this amazing STORY. I saw this gorgeous girl trotting to her car in a little miniskirt. The back flipped up and she wasn't wearing any panties!

I think I'm going to go PUNCH the wall.

JUNE 6, 2005

CLEAR SKIES OF FRUSTRATION

It's beautiful. When's the storm coming?

The thunderstorms NEVER came.

I keep waiting! I can't tell if the ROOF is fixed if it WON'T RAIN!

JUNE 7, 2005

BIKE

I SORT of have to POOP.

Oh well.

CLICK

I'm SURE the bicycle will hold it IN.

JUNE 8, 2005

BRUSH THE CAT

Good girl!

BRUSH BRUSH

what a thick mat of fur!

Amy! Eli! Look at the thick mat of fur I got from brushing Spandy!

I made it into a little toupee for her.

JUNE 9, 2005

VERMONT BLOGGERS HAVE A
GEEK PARTY

It's a lap top!

I have one too!

Pat Pat

Eli's learned to say "Blog"

Bog!

Do you think the popular kids will come and...

Beat us up?

JUNE 10, 2005

I SUFFER

AT FIRST I WAS EXCITED TO SEE ALL THE GIRLS IN BIKINIS.

THEN I GOT DEPRESSED.

Sigh

LATER

Why are you being such a jerk?

My knee hurts

JUNE 11, 2005

NEW & CUTE

I love your cute new haircut. I want to have sex with you every single day from now on...

...until the novelty wears off.

I guess I should try to ration it to preserve the novelty as long as possible, then.

JUNE 12, 2005

MONDAY MORNING AND THE PUBLIC UNVEILING
HUMIDITY & HUMANITY

My new haircut is already ruined!

It must be the humidity.

You really think it's ruined?

It looked good for a couple days

LATER

My brain's all thick & soggy

JUNE 13, 2005

FORGE AHEAD

ONE MILE THROUGH THE POURING RAIN WITH A LOOK OF GRIM DETERMINATION:

GRUNT

Man, this is incredibly difficult.

The difficulty is making me happy.

JUNE 14, 2005

OUCHY TOMATO

Could you put the rest of this tomato back in the fridge for me?

Ow!

The tomato hurt you?!

No...

...Eli just stepped on my foot.

JUNE 15, 2005

BREAKFAST WITH R2

Do you like having breakfast with R2D2?

yyeSSSss!

D2!

DINNER WITH DECLAN

Declan is coming over tonight to play with you and daddy.

Gluck Gluck! *

boo? **

* DECLAN

** SHOES

JUNE 16, 2005

BIG RAIN

Maybe I should pull over.

why?!

to wait till the rain stops.

it's NOT GOING to stop!

JUNE 17, 2005

BUNNY BUCKLER

buckle the bunny up.

Yup, gotta buckle up the bunny.
CLICK

We don't want him to hop away!

hop hop!

JUNE 18, 2005

DADDIES DAY

Happy Father's Day!
SHAKE
TOOT

SHAKE SHAKE
TOOT
TOOT

TOOT
Hi

WHACK

JUNE 19, 2005

AWESOME COMICS

Are you going to draw an awesome comic about us recording this song? *

I don't know
Come on! Nothing more important happened today!

EARLIER
Something fell out of the sky and hit me on the head

Quick! Run down the street yelling "The sky is falling!"

* SUPERF*CKERS THEME

JUNE 20, 2005

CITY RASH

JASON'S VISITING FROM NEW YORK CITY

Look at my hands

They were all poison-ivy but now they're getting better.

Geez!

How did you get poison ivy in the city?

I think I got it from a second-hand computer keyboard at work.

JUNE 21, 2005

COLD SUN

I'm going to go outside to eat my sandwich and drink my juice.

It's cold!

Maybe it'll be warmer if I stand in the SUN.

Nope.

JUNE 22, 2005

UPDATE:

YESTERDAY:

BURP

I feel awful

I guess when I drew today's strip about the sandwich I jumped the gun a little. I should've waited to draw about how sick the sandwich made me.

You can draw an update tomorrow.

JUNE 23, 2005

CHARLOTTE, NORTH CAROLINA
EYE BITER

Sluurp... ow! I think I got a piece of ice in my eye.

That's O.K, it'll melt.

Now I think it was a bug. It moved over here.

AFTER REMOVING THE BUG I RETURNED TO MY HOTEL AND EXAMINED THE EYE. THERE'S A LARGE PUFFY AREA, AND WHEN I LOOK AROUND, THE SURFACE OF MY EYE WRINKLES.

BULGE

WRINKLE

IT ITCHES.

JUNE 24, 2005
"HEROES CON"

SEPERATION INSANITY

THINKING OF AMY.

LATELY WHEN I TELL HER "I LOVE YOU" I'M NOT SURE THE DEPTH OF MY FEELING IS REALLY GETTING THROUGH.

There must be some way to say it.

DRUNK ON DRINK TICKETS IN THE ELEVATOR TO THE 17th FLOOR IN THE WESTIN HOTEL:

ARE YOU insane?

HEROES CON
CHARLOTTE, NC

JUNE 25, 2005

SUMMER SNOW

Tree fluff.

TREMBLY'S FAN

Robot! Hi R2D2!

JUNE 26, 2005

HOT NAP

AND SO, THE POWER, IT WENT OUT...

AND THERE'S NO FAN FOR ELI'S NAP

JUNE 27, 2005

Eli, don't stand still! The mosquitos will bite you!

SLAP

WAAA

OOPS

Oh, honey! I'm not mad at you. I was just hitting the mosquitto.

ha ha! SLAP

JUNE 28, 2005

PROFESSOR PANIC

DRAW FASTER

I can't control this class... it's chaos!

POUND

hey... I smell pizza!

AFTER LUNCH

I am a master!

THIS IS WORKING PERFECTLY

JUNE 29, 2005

CORDUROY SUMMER

Aren't you really hot in your corduroys?

Well... I'm really hot...

...but I don't know WHAT I'm in.

JUNE 30, 2005

ANNIVERSARY

You know, I can very clearly remember the first time I told you I love you.

oh yeah? When was that.

It was the summer of 1986 and you were 16 years old.

And you loved me?

Yes.

JULY 1, 2005

LUCKY DAYS

YESTERDAY:

Somehow when I tied my shoe I ended up with three loops.

Today's your lucky day!

I DIDN'T UNTIE MY SHOES WHEN I TOOK THEM OFF LAST NIGHT OR WHEN I PUT THEM BACK ON TODAY.

Today's my lucky day too.

JULY 2, 2005

YIN YANG YORF

...I could have my forehead removed.

Then your eyebrows would touch your hairline.

That's true!

Where would my brain go? Squished to the back of my head?

Down into your throat.

Gurgle

JULY 3, 2005

EXPATRIOTS

Do you think the border guard will be mad that we went to Canada on the 4th of July?

Why do you know people from Canada?

JULY 4, 2005

Let's go look at the Rain

See?

JULY 5, 2005

UNIQUE

?

I've never seen a bug quite like that before.

I suppose I shouldn't kill it.

JULY 6, 2005

FLIGHT

MY SHOULDER BLADES ITCH WITH INSECT POISON.

ermf

SCRATCH

I IMAGINE GROWING MOSQUITTO WINGS...

AND I FLY TO SAN FRANCISCO.

JULY 7, 2005

ICON 4

ILLUSTRATION CONFERENCE, SAN FRANCISCO

Well... I don't want to be mean to all the illustrators out there ... But illustration is NOT art. It's just a job. It's like making chairs or something.

Comics are art, but not illustration.

hee-hee

boo!

hisss

hisss

booo!

hissss

JULY 8, 2005

GOODBYE, SAN FRANCISCO

BUILDINGS DISAPPEARING INTO FOG.

WET AIR WITH INVISIBLE STINGING RAIN.

TINGLE

AN OLD FRIEND FROM HIGH SCHOOL, TRANSFORMING HIS GENDER.

MY ROOM ON THE 22ND FLOOR, SO SECRET IT CAN ONLY BE ACCESSED BY SWIPING MY KEY CARD IN THE ELEVATOR.

JULY 9, 2005

SLEEPY BEACH

This is the life I was meant to lead.

JULY 10, 2005

If you're wondering why I'm crawling. it's because my leg is asleep.

JULY 11, 2005

GOING TO SAN DIEGO

I don't like being away from home.

Oh, you'll have a good time.

And if you stayed here you'd just be bored and grumpy.

JULY 12, 2005

READING A NOVEL

WORDS TANGLE IN MY EYES LIKE STRANGLING AN OCTOPUS...

TWISTING INTO INCOMPREHENSIBLE KNOTS, THICKENING INTO ROPES OF MEANINGLESSNESS.

Z

JULY 13, 2005

RABBITIOUS

Oh! My bunny loves your book!

Your bunny?

She loves to sit on it.

ELSEWHERE

AMERKAN ELF

SAN DIEGO COMICON   JULY 14, 2005

PORTRAIT OF A GIRL

Could you draw a picture of me in my sketchbook?

I bet you could do me real good.

That's dirty!   Oops

Oh my

But I bet you could!

SAN DIEGO COMICON   JULY 15, 2005

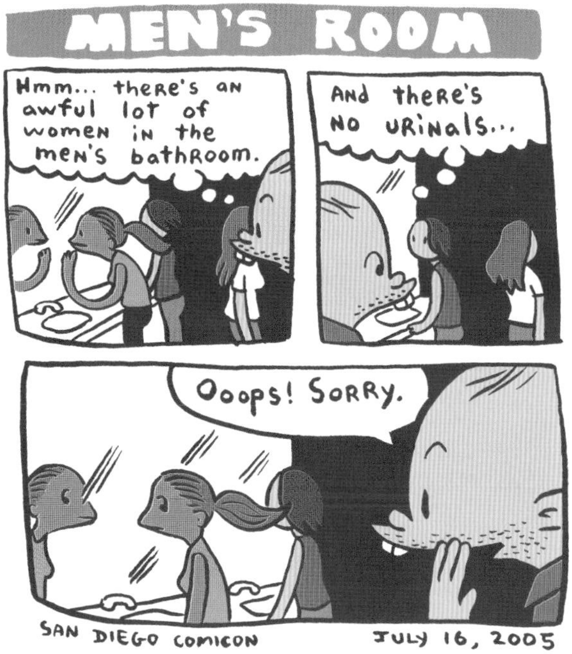
MEN'S ROOM
Hmm... there's an awful lot of women in the men's bathroom.
And there's no urinals...
Ooops! Sorry.
SAN DIEGO COMICON
JULY 16, 2005

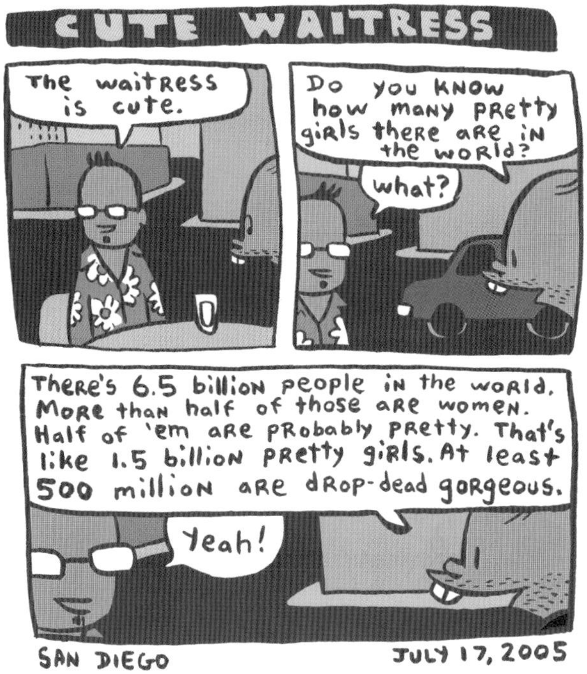
CUTE WAITRESS
The waitress is cute.
Do you know how many pretty girls there are in the world?
what?
There's 6.5 billion people in the world. More than half of those are women. Half of 'em are probably pretty. That's like 1.5 billion pretty girls. At least 500 million are drop-dead gorgeous.
Yeah!
SAN DIEGO
JULY 17, 2005

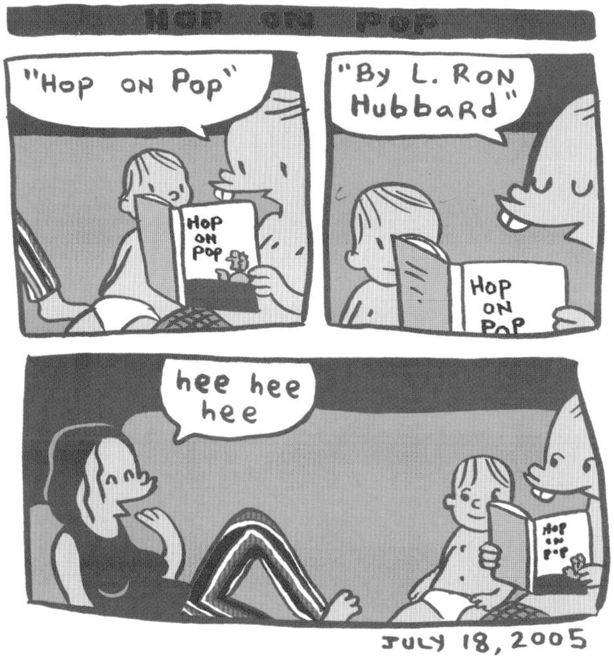
HOP ON POP
"Hop on Pop"
HOP ON POP
"By L. Ron Hubbard"
HOP ON POP
hee hee hee
HOP ON POP
JULY 18, 2005

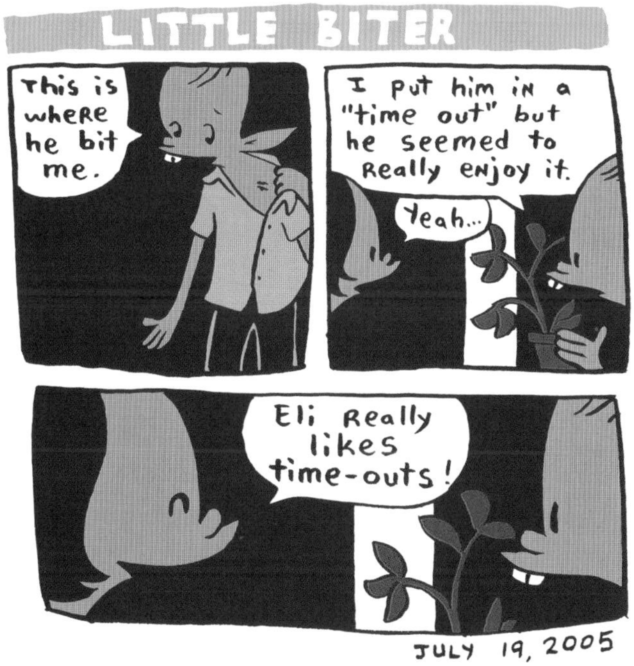
LITTLE BITER
This is where he bit me.
I put him in a "time out" but he seemed to really enjoy it.
Yeah...
Eli really likes time-outs!
JULY 19, 2005

I'VE GOT A HAT ON
AT THE BEACH

Should I go swimming with my hat on?

hee hee hee

I could use it as a Rudder!

hee hee hee ha ha

JULY 20, 2005

WEENED

Now that Eli is weened, he's not a baby anymore.

It's sad!

Sob

Don't worry... he still wears diapers.

Thank God

?

JULY 21, 2005

CHOCOLATE TEMPTATION

chocolate

I wonder what it would be like if I stepped on it?

Like a turd.

JULY 22, 2005

CRICKETS

Listen to the crickets!

VROOOM

The crickets are driving a car!

JULY 23, 2005

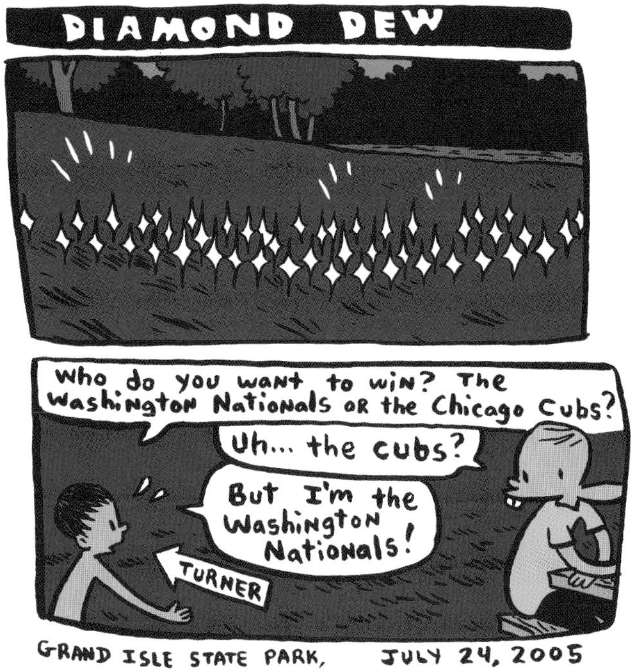
DIAMOND DEW
Who do you want to win? The Washington Nationals or the Chicago Cubs?
Uh... the cubs?
But I'm the Washington Nationals!
TURNER
GRAND ISLE STATE PARK, JULY 24, 2005

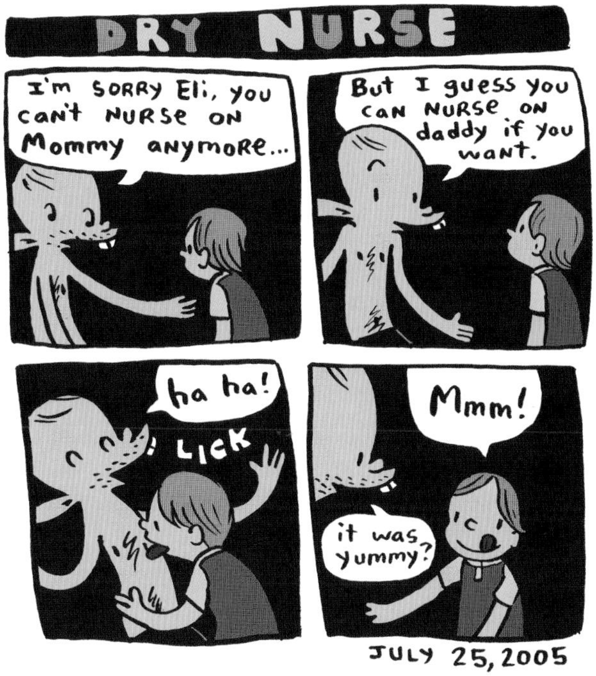
DRY NURSE
I'm SORRY Eli, you can't NURSE ON Mommy anymore...
But I guess you can NURSE ON daddy if you want.
ha ha!
LICK
Mmm!
it was yummy?
JULY 25, 2005

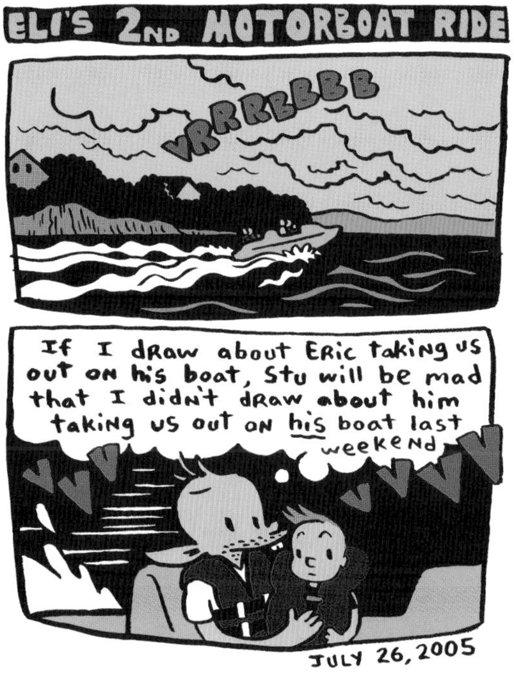
ELI'S 2ND MOTORBOAT RIDE
VRRRBBBB
If I draw about Eric taking us out on his boat, Stu will be mad that I didn't draw about him taking us out on his boat last weekend
JULY 26, 2005

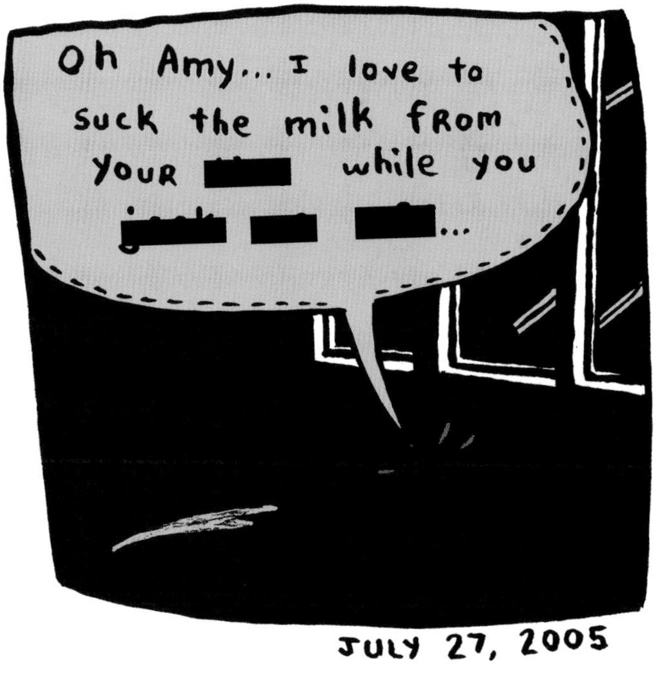
Oh Amy... I love to suck the milk from your [redacted] while you [redacted] [redacted] [redacted]...
JULY 27, 2005

FLASH FEELING

I RAN UPSTAIRS AND READ A BOOK

Eli made me so mad!

then he hurt my feelings

JULY 28, 2005

CAR NAP

Are you falling asleep too?

I would be...

but thinking about the mosquitto bite I just got is keeping me awake

JULY 29, 2005

MAKING AMY MAD

Amy, is this a bug bite on my chin?

It itches

I don't KNOW!

You're mad at me?!!

why?

THROB

JULY 30, 2005

SICK OF IT

Spandy threw up on my swim suit.

STILL ANGRY ABOUT A CROQUET GAME.

Gah

TWENTY MINUTES LATER

That is disgusting!

I didn't want to clean it up till after dinner.

Ask the vet to put her to sleep tomorrow

JULY 31, 2005

SLEEPING BEAUTY

AUGUST 1, 2005

SUPER SUMMERZ

AUGUST 2, 2005

IT LINGERED IN MY MIND TODAY THAT I
THREW A PEN ACROSS THE ROOM YESTERDAY.

I NEVER HIDE MY EMOTIONS.

AUGUST 3, 2005

WE'RE ALL GETTING FAMOUS

AFTER THE
GOGOL BORDELLO SHOW

AUGUST 4, 2005

GRANDPA'S KNOB

DRESSING UP FOR MY ART OPENING *

* AT THE BRATTLEBORO MUSEUM OF ART

AUGUST 5, 2005

POOOOOOOO!

AUGUST 6, 2005

LITTLE BACK ROOM

AUGUST 7, 2005

TEETH IN THE NIGHT

AUGUST 8, 2005

THIRD PERSON

IN A REST ROOM IN MONTREAL

Daddy's going to wash his hands.

I mean, Daddy's going to wash my hands.

I mean, I'm going to wash Daddy's hands

Ha!

AUGUST 9, 2005

I'll change your diaper on the church lawn.

No

FLAP

After I change you, you can RUN and play.

Oh... I forgot to bring any diapers with us.

AUGUST 10, 2005

SHREK BALL

Snort

huff

fidget fidget

DOOONT

High!
High!

CATCH!

Eli! You kicked it high!

Pi-tchoo!

RaR!

AUGUST 11, 2005

HALF THIS HALF THAT

LATER:

It's unbelievable to see you up there doing that...

COLBY

...knowing that just a few hours ago I saw you changing a diaper!

AT "ONE HALF LOUNGE"

AUGUST 12, 2005

THOUSANDS OF SOUNDS

THE NIGHT IS ELECTRIC WITH INSECT TECHNO

AND THE HUM AND BUZZ OF WINE FROM THE WEDDING OF SARER & GREG

AUGUST 13, 2005

WHAT'S IN YOUR MOUTH

What's in your mouth?

A hole!

ha ha

You're right, Eli. There is a hole in there!

La

AUGUST 14, 2005

EATING COLOR

*Goppa-glee!

You want a popsicle?

A black! A black!

* GOPPAGLEE = POPSICLE

There aren't any black popsicles, but you can have a yellow one

There's no such thing as a black popsicle

A BLACK!

AUGUST 15, 2005

WEED PULLER

WHEN I BLINK MY EYES...

...I SEE WEEDS

I give up! I'm not pulling any more weeds out of the yard.

Good

SOON

Stop! No!

AUGUST 16, 2005

COUNTING YOUR PARTS

How many noses do you have?

one

...two

Theee!

AUGUST 17, 2005

COUNTING BOATS

1... 2... 3... 2
...3..2...3
2...3

...1...2
...3...2
...3...2
...3
hmm

How does Eli really pronounce "3"? I think I wrote it as "theee" yesterday.

3!
It's more like "wee", I guess

AUGUST 18, 2005

THE LETTER

There's a nasty letter to the editor about my comic strip in Seven Days*? No, I haven't seen it!

oh boy!
I can't wait to read the letter.

RUSTLE

wee!

* SEVEN DAYS IS THE LOCAL PAPER HERE THAT RUNS THIS STRIP

AUGUST 19, 2005

MY BATMAN

(AFTER ELI'S BIRTHDAY PARTY)

I love you, Bat Man

A dress!

Yup, you're wearing a dress, like Bat Man.

AUGUST 20, 2005

GIRL POWER

I love girls!*

They're adorable sexy cutie sweethearts!

Nope

We're bitches.

* WOMEN

AUGUST 21, 2005

MANA FROM HELL

I guess this piece of cheese fell out of the sky.

There's an apple core over here.

(ONCE I FOUND RAW CHICKEN IN THE BACK YARD.)

AUGUST 22, 2005

PAINTER'S PROGRESS

EARLIER IN THE SUMMER I HAD SOME PHOTOS OF ELI'S FACE PRINTED.

WEEKS LATER I BOUGHT SOME WOOD & SOME ACRYLIC PAINT. CRESTON CUT THE WOOD FOR ME AND I PRIMED IT.

GESSO

MAYBE A MONTH LATER, I FINALLY GOT STARTED. I CUT OUT ONE OF THE FACES, GLUED IT TO THE BOARD...

...AND PAINTED A MONSTER!

It's an Eli-monster!

AUGUST 23, 2005

WOMEN'S CLOTHING

pitchoo! pitchoo!
pitchoo

ha ha   pitchoo!

AUGUST 24, 2005

AUGUST 25, 2005

AUGUST 26, 2005

AUGUST 27, 2005

AUGUST 28, 2005

THE BATHING SCIENCES

Next time you should put your head back...

Like this! Then I'll pour the water on like this
Pssh!

And that way the soap won't go in your eyes.
and the water will go down the back
my CRY!

AUGUST 29, 2005

MY WIFE AND MY CAT

I MADE AMY MAD RIGHT BEFORE SHE LEFT FOR HER BOOK-CLUB MEETING.

Spandy...if you were a Magic Cat, I wouldn't have any of these problems.

I'm not magic?

AUGUST 30, 2005

TIME OUTS

Eli, I don't want to give you "time outs" any more.

So... don't just hit or kick me. Ask me "Do you want to fight?" first.

fight?
O.K!
RARR!
Kick!

AUGUST 31, 2005

IMPOSSIBILITY

Wait here... I have to go down to the basement to get your clothes
I'll be right back

What? Cat puke?! How did cat puke get in the basement? The door was shut.

Never underestimate a magic cat.

SEPTEMBER 1, 2005

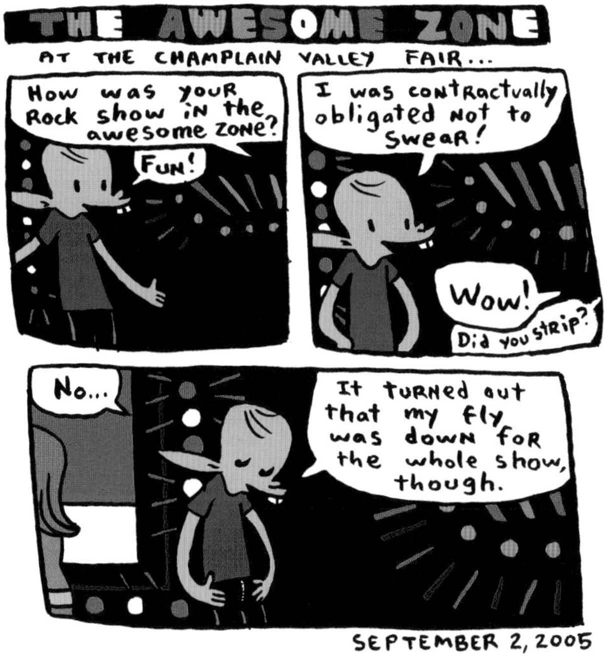
THE AWESOME ZONE
AT THE CHAMPLAIN VALLEY FAIR...
How was your Rock show in the awesome zone?
Fun!
I was contractually obligated not to swear!
Wow! Did you strip?
No...
It turned out that my fly was down for the whole show, though.
SEPTEMBER 2, 2005

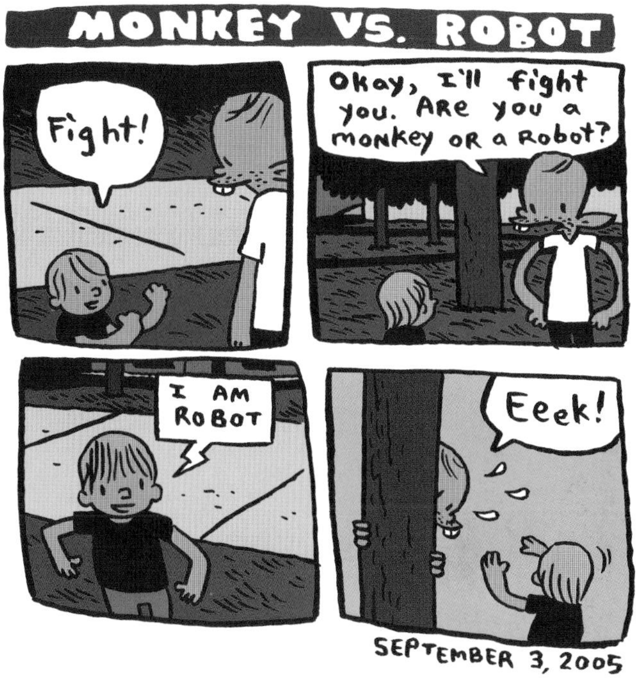
MONKEY VS. ROBOT
Fight!
Okay, I'll fight you. Are you a monkey or a robot?
I AM ROBOT
Eeek!
SEPTEMBER 3, 2005

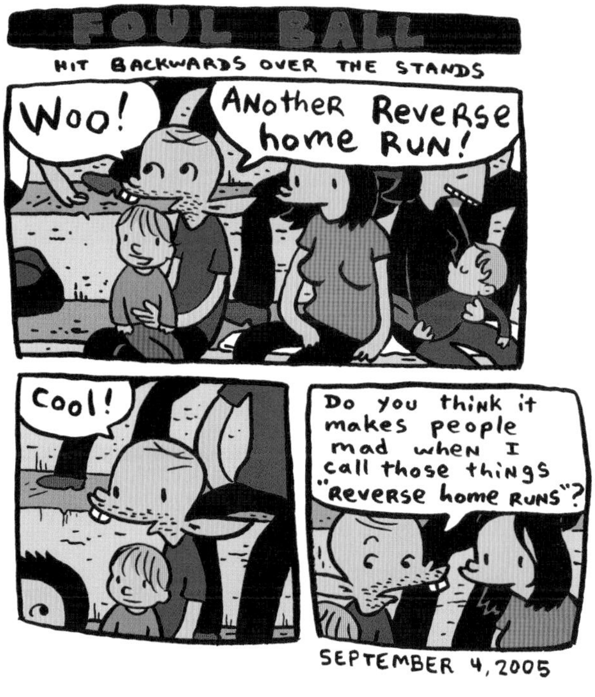
FOUL BALL
HIT BACKWARDS OVER THE STANDS
Woo!
Another Reverse home run!
Cool!
Do you think it makes people mad when I call those things "reverse home runs"?
SEPTEMBER 4, 2005

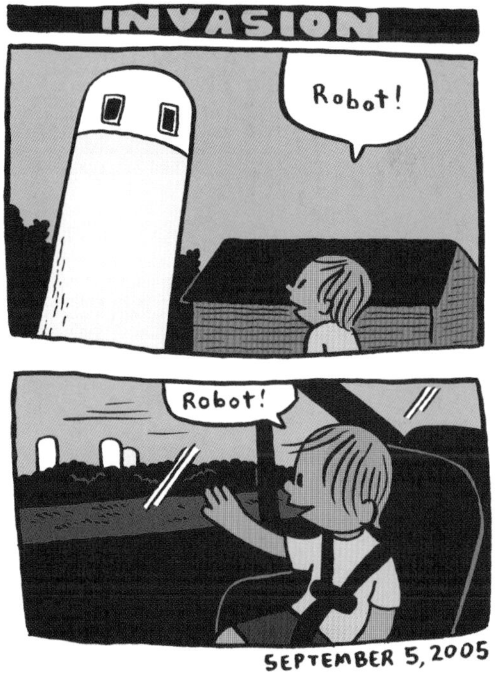
INVASION
Robot!
Robot!
SEPTEMBER 5, 2005

PAINTING A BIG ONE

This is what I have for paints

That's fine I don't think it even matters

It's bigger than I'm used to, but I'm not even scared

SEPTEMBER 6, 2005

TONGUEY

There's a thore on my tongue

thee? No! And I don't want to

SEPTEMBER 7, 2005

ICE CREAM FLOATS

The ice cream keeps coming back up the back of my throat.

I guess you've reached your limit then.

I think I could puke pure ice cream and keep the rest of the food down.

SEPTEMBER 8, 2005

GET OUT OF THE WAY

I hate commiting manslaughter

Vehicular in particular.

SEPTEMBER 9, 2005

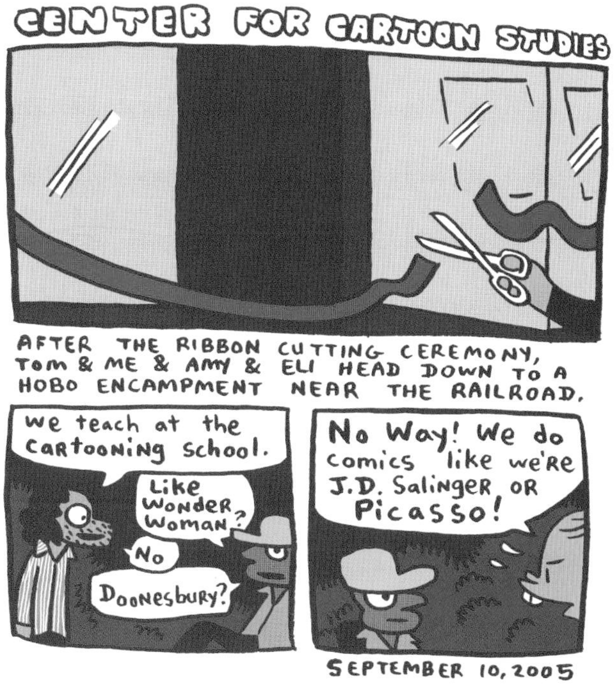
CENTER FOR CARTOON STUDIES
AFTER THE RIBBON CUTTING CEREMONY, TOM & ME & AMY & ELI HEAD DOWN TO A HOBO ENCAMPMENT NEAR THE RAILROAD.
We teach at the cartooning school.
Like Wonder Woman?
No
Doonesbury?
No Way! We do comics like we're J.D. Salinger or Picasso!
SEPTEMBER 10, 2005

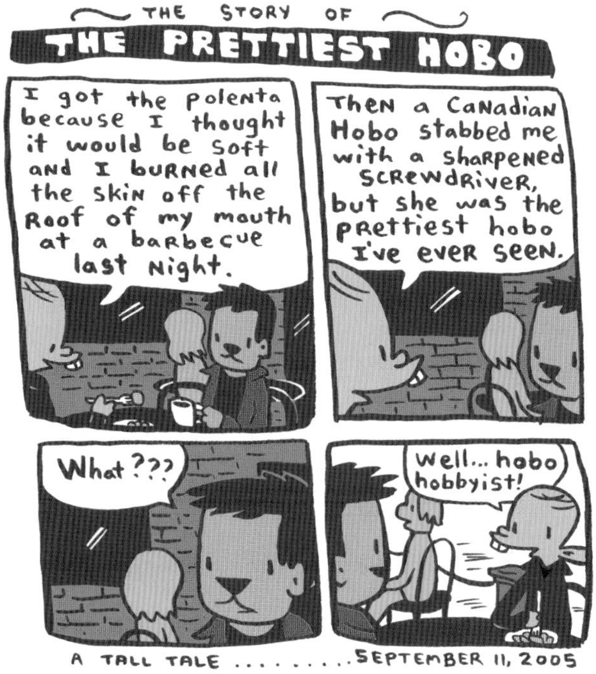
THE STORY OF
THE PRETTIEST HOBO
I got the polenta because I thought it would be soft and I burned all the skin off the roof of my mouth at a barbecue last night.
Then a Canadian Hobo stabbed me with a sharpened screwdriver, but she was the prettiest hobo I've ever seen.
What???
Well... hobo hobbyist!
A TALL TALE ....SEPTEMBER 11, 2005

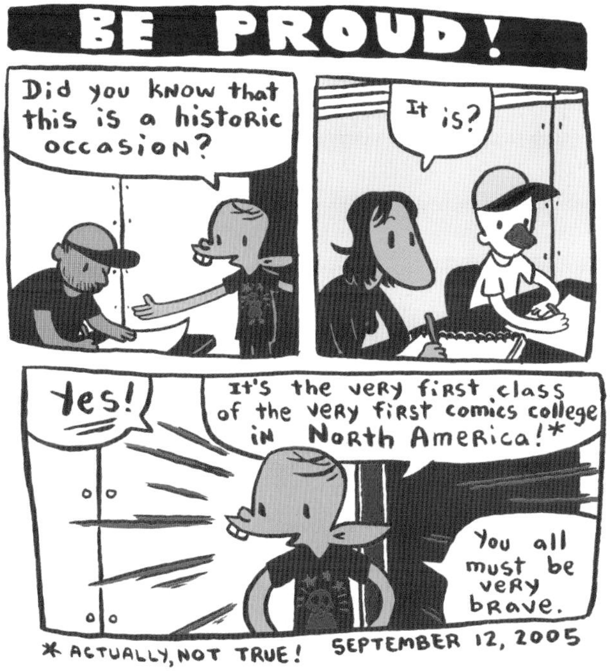
BE PROUD!
Did you know that this is a historic occasion?
It is?
Yes!
It's the very first class of the very first comics college in North America!*
You all must be very brave.
* ACTUALLY, NOT TRUE!
SEPTEMBER 12, 2005

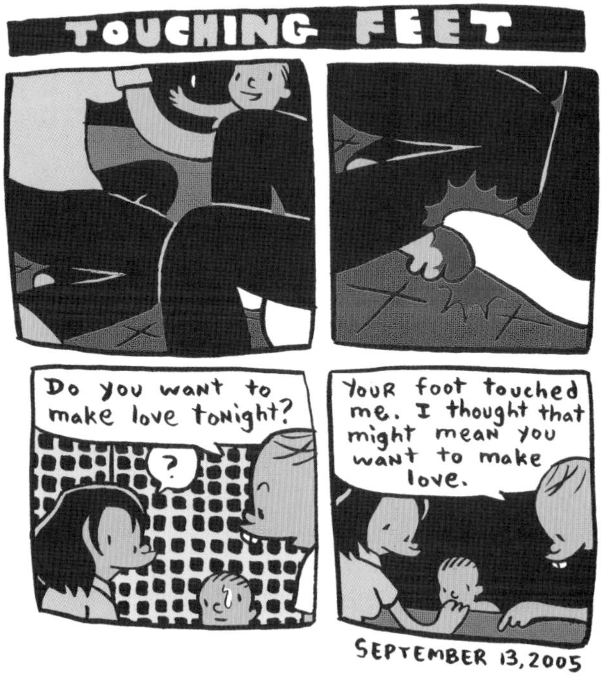
TOUCHING FEET
Do you want to make love tonight?
?
Your foot touched me. I thought that might mean you want to make love.
SEPTEMBER 13, 2005

SUMMER'S OVER

Do you want to walk mommy to work?

Yesh

You're slowing me down!

Sunflowers!

MUCH EARLIER:

I'm humping your KNEES!

SEPTEMBER 14, 2005

COUGH SYRUP INJECTION

Open your mouth and take your cough medicine!

No

Noo!

Eli

No cough!

Then you'll have to take it anally!

SEPTEMBER 15, 2005

OCEAN HAIRCUT

WOOOSH

For a brief moment I was reminded of being on a mountain by the sea and feeling the breeze

WOOSH

Here's some more ocean breeze for you

VOOSH

BLOWING AWAY THE LITTLE HAIRS

No. It was just a brief moment. It's definitely over now.

WOOSH

SEPTEMBER 16, 2005

ELF AWARE

I saw your pictures in the paper today...

... you media whore!

Hey!

LATER

Then he called me a media whore

Just for having my picture in the paper dancing with Eli.

Although, it is sorta TRUE. I knew exactly how to move to make sure that the reporter's photo turned out good...

...'cause I wanted us to be in the paper

SEPTEMBER 17, 2005

NONE OF YOUR BUSINES

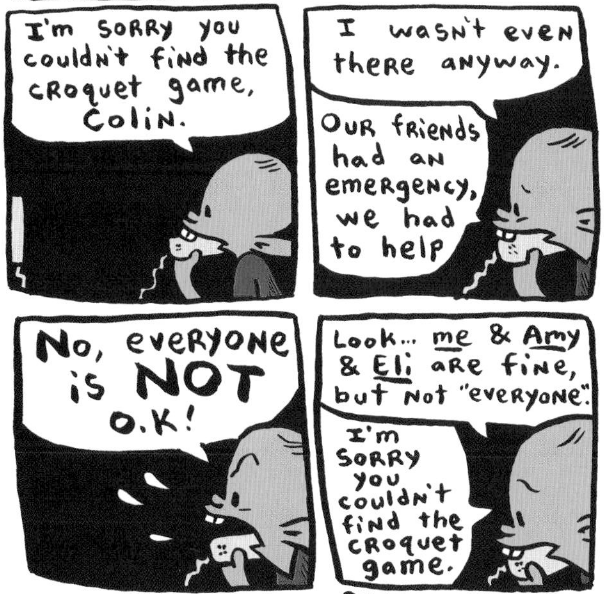
I'm sorry you couldn't find the croquet game, Colin.
I wasn't even there anyway.
Our friends had an emergency, we had to help
No, everyone is NOT O.K!
Look... me & Amy & Eli are fine, but not "everyone".
I'm sorry you couldn't find the croquet game.

SEPTEMBER 18, 2005

ACADEMIA

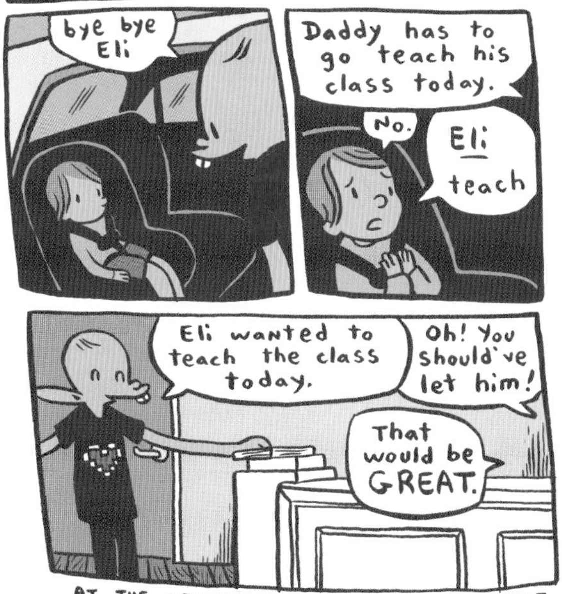
bye bye Eli
Daddy has to go teach his class today.
No.
Eli teach
Eli wanted to teach the class today.
Oh! You should've let him!
That would be GREAT.

AT THE CENTER FOR CARTOON STUDIES

SEPTEMBER 19, 2005

PRIME SUSPECT

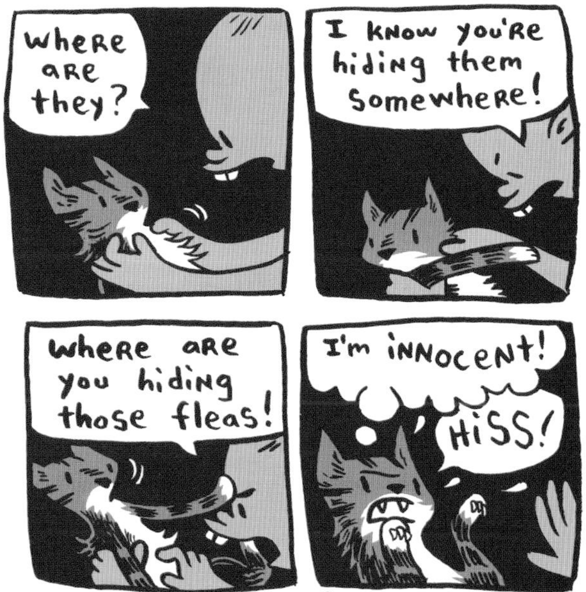
Where are they?
I know you're hiding them somewhere!
Where are you hiding those fleas!
I'm INNOCENT!
HiSS!

SEPTEMBER 20, 2005

SMALL TALK

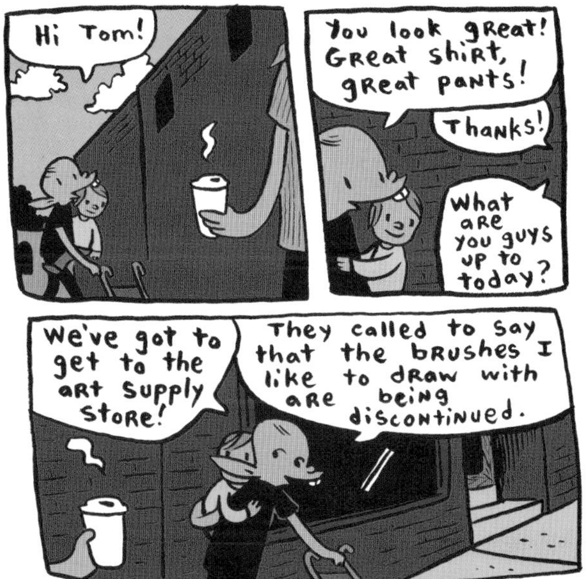
Hi Tom!
You look great! Great shirt, great pants!
Thanks!
What are you guys up to today?
We've got to get to the art supply store!
They called to say that the brushes I like to draw with are being discontinued.

SEPTEMBER 21, 2005

CUTE MONEY

Oh! I forgot you had that car accident.

Right.

So... I guess all my royalties on The Cute Manifesto are going to your medical bills?

Heh.

I'll pay you when I get the insurance settlement.

SPEAKER PHONE

YES! YES!

SEPTEMBER 22, 2005

BLUEBERRY BOMB

This splat of bird poop is so dark. The bird must've been eating blueberries.

Isn't it too late in the season for blueberries?

WIPE

Actually, this is exactly the same color as blue ball-point pen ink.

SEPTEMBER 23, 2005

TOUCHING

AT THE BURLINGTON LITERARY FESTIVAL

Does anybody have a cell phone I can use?

Sure.

Thanks

There's something yucky on the button... I don't want to touch it.

SEPTEMBER 24, 2005

SOUNDS

shuff shuff

chuff kfff

Did I hear the cat starting to throw up?

SEPTEMBER 25, 2005

JIM DOUGLAS

The governor is coming to our class today.

Really?

He's late

He's late he's late he's late he's late he's late late late

Maybe he's trying to time it so he'll be here for the nude model!

Ha!

ho

AT THE CENTER FOR CARTOON STUDIES

SEPTEMBER 26, 2005

BUS TRIP

LAST NIGHT, RIDING THE BUS BACK TO BURLINGTON, I STARTED TO HALLUCINATE.

I TRIED TO TAKE NOTES, BUT...

it's too much.

SEPTEMBER 27, 2005

ONWARD HUMAN BEINGS

My hip hurts.

That's too bad

It's hurt for like ten years, off and on. I think it's an injury from doing high kicks with my band.

Plus, I walk way way too fast.

But I think there might also be a psychological component...

This latest bout began the moment I heard that Mary's husband might need a hip replacement.

SEPTEMBER 28, 2005

YOU CAN'T STOP US

It's WIIINDY!

WOOO!

And now it's LESS WINDY

WOO!

And you're UGLY, lady!

Ha!

SEPTEMBER 29, 2005

SEPTEMBER 30, 2005

OCTOBER 1, 2005

OCTOBER 2, 2005

OCTOBER 3, 2005

YELLOW BEAR AND THE SHINY PENNY

Bat Man?

Oh, honey. I'm sick of telling Bat Man stories

Can I tell you a story about Yellow Bear?

No Yellow Bear

BAT MAN

Please? The Yellow Bear story has a PENNY in it.

a penny?

Yes!

OCTOBER 4, 2005

RING BOX

Why is it so worn out?

EVERY NIGHT FOR TEN YEARS I'VE PUT MY WEDDING RING BACK IN THE BOX BEFORE GOING TO SLEEP. (MY REASON IS THAT IF I EVER GET REALLY FAT I DON'T WANT TO END UP WITH THE RING STUCK ON MY FINGER). THE VELVET HAS WORN OFF THE SPOTS I TOUCH THE MOST:

OCTOBER 5, 2005

Is it okay if I tell people?

What?

Random House is going to publish James' children's book.

Oh, Fuck you

OCTOBER 6, 2005

WHITE BLOB ON A FUZZY TOWEL

I think I'm going to throw up

cough

Oh!

Sweetie, I didn't know milk becomes a solid blob inside your tummy

OCTOBER 7, 2005

ENJOY THE JOY

I'M SO SICK OF MY CONSTANT MOOD SWINGS UP & DOWN ALL DAY LONG. IT'S EXHAUSTING. I ENJOY THE JOY BUT THE DARKNESS IS SHARP.

Rain drops!

Ha ha

GAH! The Raindrops BURN

MY APOLOGY

AFTER YELLING AT MY MOM AND AMY

I'm SORRY you hate me.

I don't hate you!

OCTOBER 8, 2005

MY POOR MOM

I shouldn't have yelled at my mom yesterday. She just drives me crazy.

I better call her and apologize

BEEP BOOP

SOON

blah blah blah NONSENSE NONSENSE

OCTOBER 9, 2005

TALKY TALK

THE LAST DAY OF MY CLASS:

blah blah blah blah blah blah blah

blah bla blah dee blah

Um... I don't know if this rambling monologue about my work is useful to anyone

It's funny!

THE CENTER FOR CARTOON STUDIES

OCTOBER 10, 2005

THE DOCTOR'S ROOM

How should I describe how my hip feels?

Does it hurt?

Who knows?

SHRUG

OCTOBER 11, 2005

KRAZY & IGNATZ

STEP ONE: WIPE UP THE CAT PUKE WITH A PAPER TOWEL.

STEP TWO: SCRUB THE SPOT WITH DISH DETERGENT AND WATER.

STEP THREE: PLACE A FOLDED PAPER TOWEL ON TOP OF THE WET SPOT AND PLACE A BRICK ON TOP OF THE PAPER TOWEL.

CONCLUSION: THIS IS WHY ALL MY IGNATZ AWARDS SMELL LIKE CAT PUKE.

OCTOBER 12, 2005

A TWO YEAR OLD'S GUYS *

"Hi" What's this guy's Name?

Um...

Tupac Toujours!

* MEXICAN WRESTLERS

OCTOBER 13, 2005

SIGNED AND NUMBERED

I SIGN & NUMBER A COUPLE HUNDRED PRINTS, ON PETER'S KITCHEN TABLE.

FART

ha ha!

My beer is right there but there's No time to drink it.

BRIDGEPORT, CT

OCTOBER 14, 2005

WEDDING SPARKLERS

FSSHH

FWSSS

The sparklers are sparkin' For Dani and Tarquin

STAMFORD, CT

OCTOBER 15, 2005

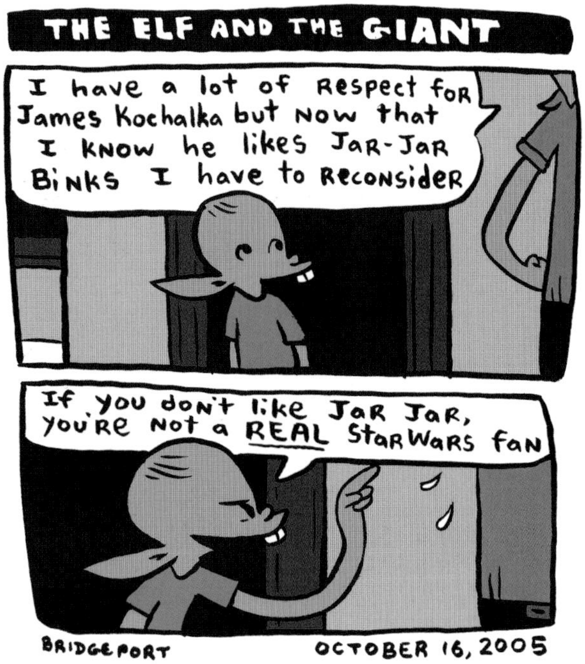
THE ELF AND THE GIANT
I have a lot of respect for James Kochalka but now that I know he likes Jar-Jar Binks I have to reconsider
If you don't like Jar Jar, you're not a REAL Star Wars fan
BRIDGEPORT
OCTOBER 16, 2005

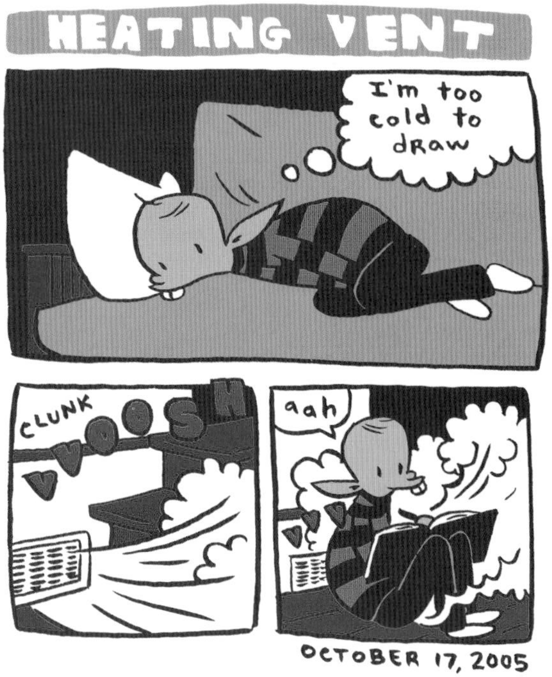
HEATING VENT
I'm too cold to draw
CLUNK
VVOOSH
aah
OCTOBER 17, 2005

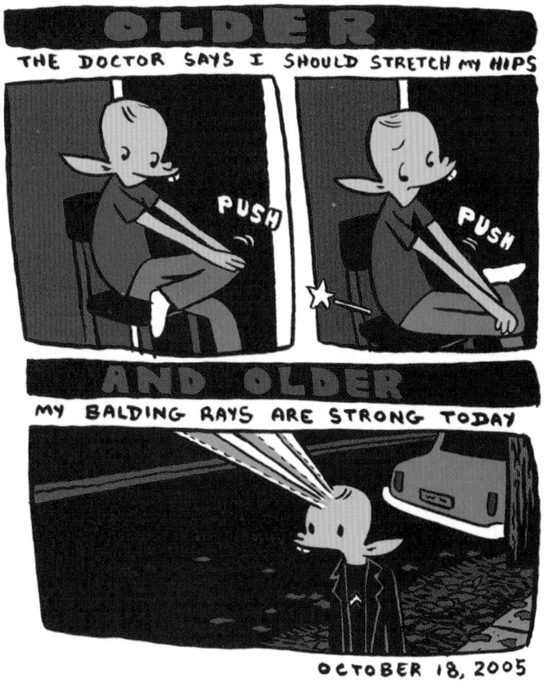
OLDER
THE DOCTOR SAYS I SHOULD STRETCH MY HIPS
PUSH
PUSH
AND OLDER
MY BALDING RAYS ARE STRONG TODAY
OCTOBER 18, 2005

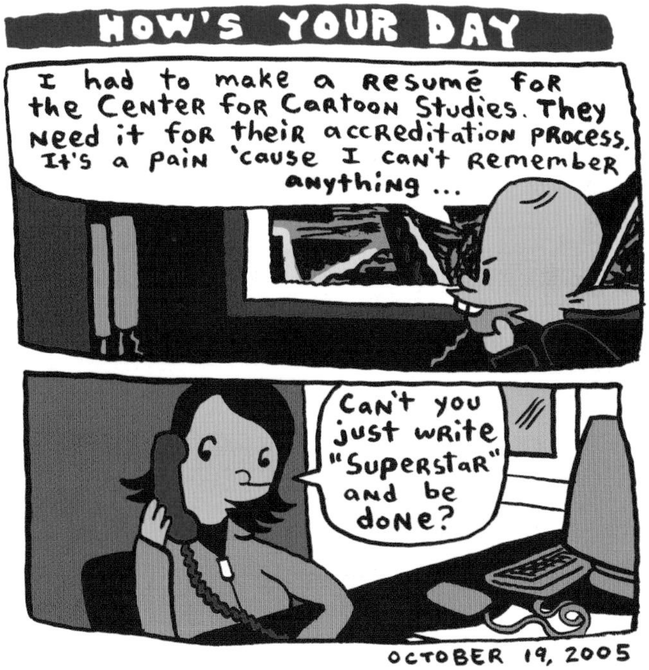
HOW'S YOUR DAY
I had to make a resumé for the Center for Cartoon Studies. They need it for their accreditation process. It's a pain 'cause I can't remember anything...
Can't you just write "Superstar" and be done?
OCTOBER 19, 2005

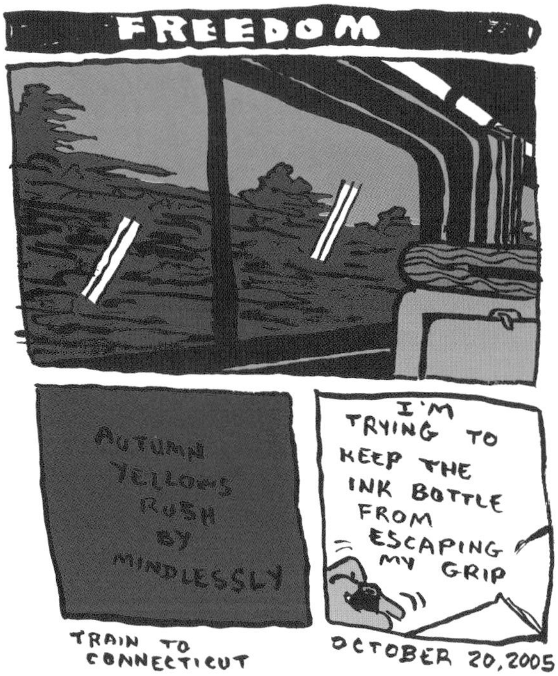
FREEDOM
AUTUMN YELLOWS RUSH BY MINDLESSLY
I'M TRYING TO KEEP THE INK BOTTLE FROM ESCAPING MY GRIP
TRAIN TO CONNECTICUT
OCTOBER 20, 2005

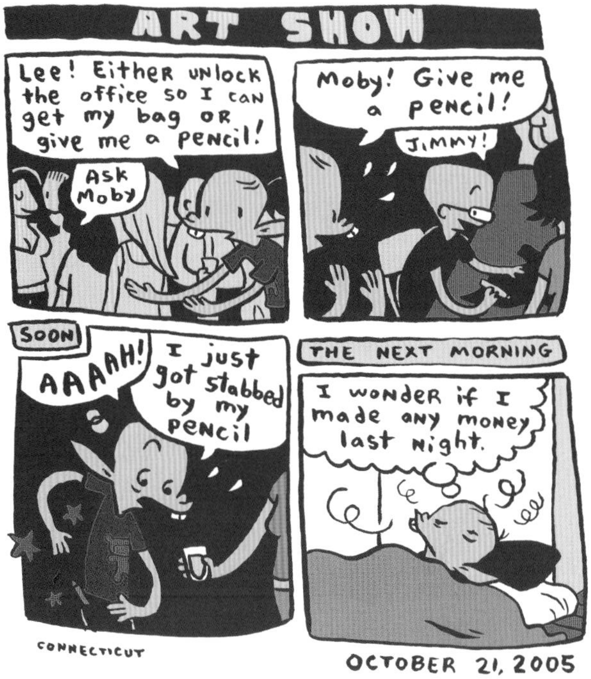
ART SHOW
Lee! Either unlock the office so I can get my bag or give me a pencil!
Ask Moby
Moby! Give me a pencil!
JIMMY!
SOON
AAAAH!
I just got stabbed by my pencil
THE NEXT MORNING
I wonder if I made any money last night.
CONNECTICUT
OCTOBER 21, 2005

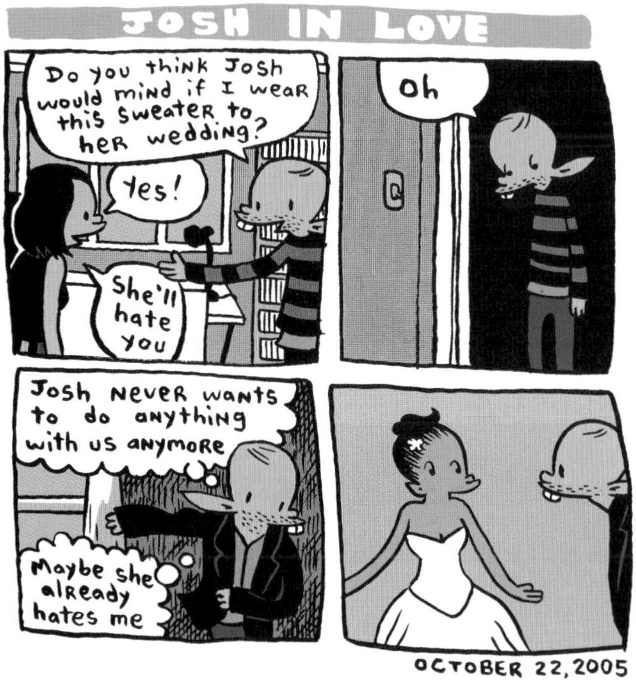
JOSH IN LOVE
Do you think Josh would mind if I wear this sweater to her wedding?
Yes!
She'll hate you
Oh
Josh never wants to do anything with us anymore
Maybe she already hates me
OCTOBER 22, 2005

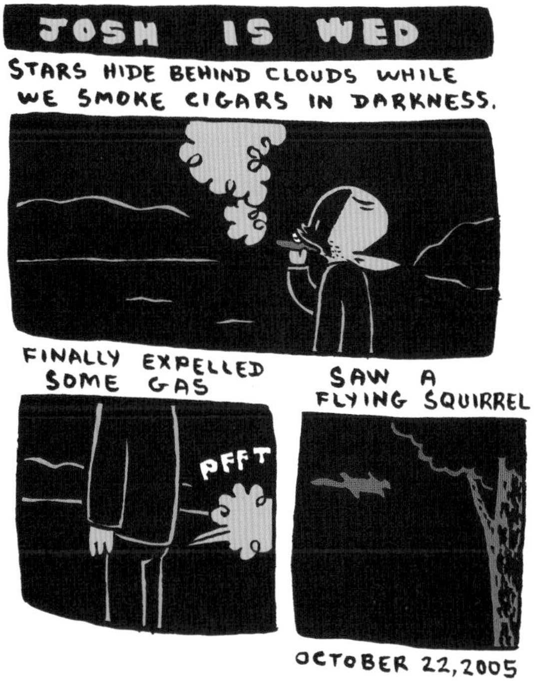
JOSH IS WED
STARS HIDE BEHIND CLOUDS WHILE WE SMOKE CIGARS IN DARKNESS.
FINALLY EXPELLED SOME GAS
PFFT
SAW A FLYING SQUIRREL
OCTOBER 22, 2005

BLOODY KNUCKLES

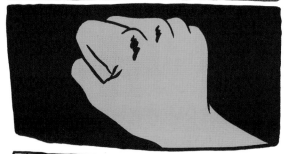

Lick suck

LICK THE FIST!

It's blueberry pie filling!

OCTOBER 23, 2005

ME ME ME

why do you have to be so hard to get along with?

I'm not hard to get along with. Everyone loves me!

They love you IN SPITE OF the fact you're hard to get along with.

Ha!

OCTOBER 24, 2005

STUCK THERE IN THE RAIN

leaf there leaf!

What?

Oh yes. There's a leaf stuck there

OCTOBER 25, 2005

YESTERDAY'S LEAF

..Just needs a little resolution.

OCTOBER 26, 2005

EVERY SO OFTEN, JASON COMES BACK FROM NYC AND WE GO OUT TO LUNCH

Bye Jason

It was nice to see you

Eli... let's put your hands in your pockets

OCTOBER 27, 2005

BATMAN'S DIAPER

Alright Batman, let's change your diaper

And this is the Bat Powder

Bat Pow der

PUFF

OCTOBER 28, 2005

PUMPKIN PURCHASE

That's a 5 dollar pumpkin and that one's from the 3 dollar section.

OR maybe it's the other way around.

We've also got another 3 dollar one outside

OCTOBER 29, 2005

WE WENT TO SEE "EVERYTHING IS ILLUMINATED"

NOTHING WAS ILLUMINATED

You can have a refund or free passes.

I want a refund AND free passes. We wasted a lot of time and had to get a baby-sitter.

I can't give out random free passes.

It's not random

It's not our fault the projector broke.

Of course it is. Maintaining the projector is the theater's responsibility

But the motors burn out all the time.

It's still the theater's responsibility

But I don't have the authority.

Well, let's talk to someone who does.

But I'd have to call the owner.

Do you have a PHONE?

Well... it worked, but I didn't like fighting about it.

Thanks for sticking up for us.

OCTOBER 30, 2005

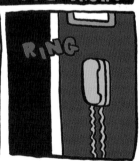

RESCUE MISSION

Where's Amy?

She's at home, handing out candy

Well, that's No FUN! We've got to go get her!

Oh, could we?

We should!

OCTOBER 31, 2005

A LITTLE BIT PSYCHIC

WHEN THE PHONE RINGS I LIKE TO TRY AND GUESS WHO'S CALLING.

RING RING

I've got No idea who it is

hello? Wait, what? Who do you think you're calling?

A WRONG NUMBER!

CLICK

NOVEMBER 1, 2005

THE LESSON

And you sit on the potty like this

Eli! You made a Poo-Poo!

You REALLY did it!

Oh!

NOVEMBER 2, 2005

TONIGHT'S THE NIGHT

Maybe I should go see a movie tonight. MIRRORMASK?

RING

I'm SORRY I won't be able to come to your Rock show tonight.

I have a ROCK show tonight?!

NOVEMBER 3, 2005

NAKED MEMORIES

LAST NIGHT AT MY ROCK SHOW AT ONE HALF

Is Amy still beautiful?
Yes!
She is.

Did you see that girl I was talking to? I went on "Spring Break" with her 16 years ago!
Did you get naked?

Actually, yes! We took naked showers together and ran down the beach naked.
Good thing Amy's not here

Actually, Amy was there naked too!
Woah!

NOVEMBER 4, 2005

KINDLING

Hi.

Hi! Do you want to help me collect sticks?

No

NOVEMBER 5, 2005

TRYING TO LEARN
TO PEE IN THE POTTY

Come out!

Come out!

Not working

NOVEMBER 6, 2005

WHAT DO DADDIES DO

I drew our kitty!

See... Spandy's on the Big Bed and there's the striped pillow...

And I also did this drawing of a Robot.

Robot pick UP kitty?

NOVEMBER 7, 2005

LIFE DRAWING

IT TOOK ME ABOUT SIX HOURS TO DO YESTERDAY'S DIARY STRIP.

I DREW THINGS AND ERASED THEM. I COULDN'T FIND THE RIGHT THING. NOTHING WAS RIGHT.

IF EVERY DAY WERE LIKE THIS I WOULD HAVE TO DIE.

← TELEVISION

NOVEMBER 8, 2005

KICK THE MOON

I kick the MOON!

BOOM

Oh! I broke it!

NOVEMBER 9, 2005

I SNUGGLE

STOMP

Eli! Don't kick your toy anymore or I'll take it away from you.

I snuggle!

NOVEMBER 10, 2005

MY SPANDY COMPANION

Spandy!

Sit on my lap to keep me warm while I draw

NOVEMBER 11, 2005

GROCERY STORY

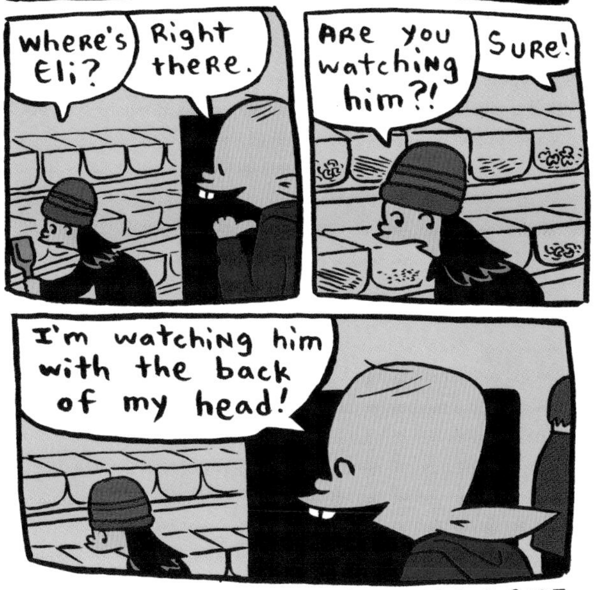
Where's Eli?
Right there.
Are you watching him?!
Sure!
I'm watching him with the back of my head!

NOVEMBER 12, 2005

A LOVELY SUNDAY

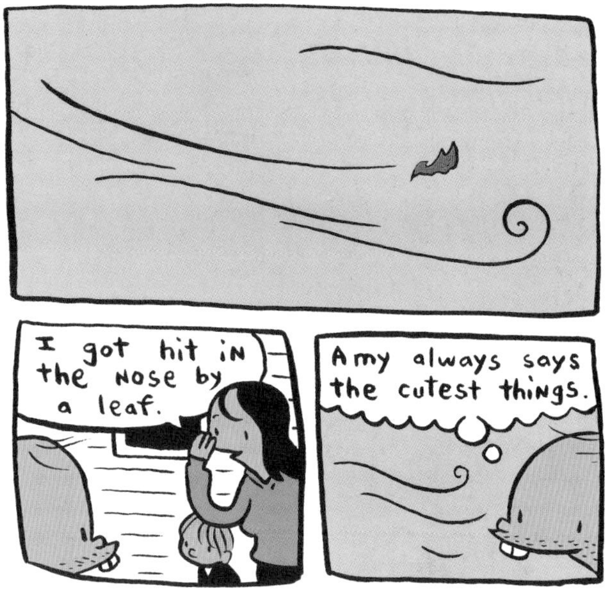
I got hit in the nose by a leaf.
Amy always says the cutest things.

NOVEMBER 13, 2005

CALLING SPANDY

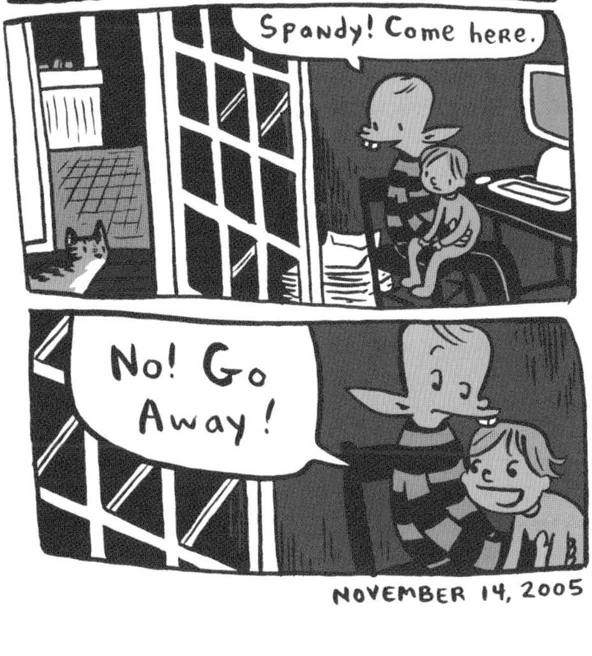
Spandy! Come here.
No! Go Away!

NOVEMBER 14, 2005

COLD & WET & QUITE HAPPY

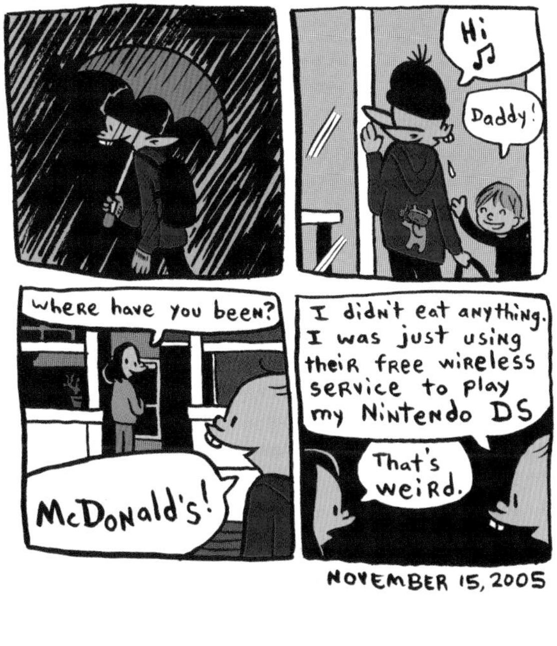
Hi ♫
Daddy!
Where have you been?
McDonald's!
I didn't eat anything. I was just using their free wireless service to play my Nintendo DS
That's weird.

NOVEMBER 15, 2005

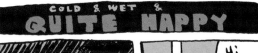

WIND IN THE HAIR,

SQUISHY GISHES 'ROUND THE FEET

Watch out, it's wet there

SQUISH

GISH

NOVEMBER 16, 2005

SILLY - STUFF

Fisticuffs?

Sippy-cup?

Not "sippy cup," **Fisticuffs!**

Cuppy-poop!

NOVEMBER 17, 2005

LITTLE SNOW

ALL SUMMER LONG ELI TALKED ABOUT THE SNOWMAN WE MADE LAST WINTER.

It snowed a little, but not enough to make a snowman.

NO NO NO NO! BIG SNOW!

I'm sure a big snow will come soon.

NOVEMBER 18, 2005

CO - AUTHORED

You know how I draw those comic strips about Eli and Mommy and Daddy?

Yesss

Well... what should I draw about today?

Um...

Eli!

NOVEMBER 19, 2005

FIGHT

I'm not fighting with you, you're fighting with me!

and you're making that smug little smile just to make me mad!

LATER

Do you want to slit my throat?

'Cause you can go ahead and do it if you want to it's alright with me. I don't mind.

NOVEMBER 20, 2005

STORY REQUESTS

Batman story and Robin

Yellow bear penny.

Yellow bear sugar castle

NOVEMBER 21, 2005

LOOKING

Let me see you!

You have SNOW ON YOUR tail. Yes you do!

NOVEMBER 22, 2005

TEENIE TINY THIRSTY TIME

I should start a juice company and sell honey-dew melon juice. I'd call it "Honey Dude's Melon Juice".

MY SISTER

ME

Ha ha ha hee hee hee ha ha hee hee SNICKER SNICKER hee hee hee.

PROUD OF MYSELF

It's funny how teeny-tiny all mom and dad's glasses are.

It's hard to ever get enough to drink.

NOVEMBER 23, 2005

MY THANKSGIVINGWEAR

Oh Damn it!
?!

I forgot to bring any changes of underwear

I forgot to bring any underwear.
Ssssfff!

NOVEMBER 24, 2005

..... MOTHER CLUTTER

Mom! Why do you save old candy wrappers? I'm throwing these away.

Ew! Here's an old dusty piece of chocolate. I'm throwing this away too.
No!

Give it to me!!
No, you don't want it! It's disgusting!

No, I LIKE it! Mmm-mmm.
Yummy.

NOVEMBER 25, 2005

JASON'S DILEMNA

Ugh. No paper towels. I'm so stupid.

How am I supposed to dry my hands?

I'll use my hair.

(LAST NIGHT AT THE BENIFIT CONCERT FOR HIS MEDICAL EXPENSES)

NOVEMBER 26, 2005

WALKING TALL

Are you okay up there?
Eli?

What? I can't hear you.
Eli?

You don't want to talk? Well... if you're O.K. just pat me on the head.

PAT PAT
Good!

NOVEMBER 27, 2005

SLEEPY TIME

WORRIES FROM MY COLLECTION

CONTRACT ISSUES
HOCKEY MONKEY
legal problems
FRIENDS

T.V. deal
MOVIE DEAL
Pinky & Stinky
MONKEY VS. ROBOT
VIDEO GAME DEAL

tax questions
TRADEMARK PROBLEMS
book deals
TIME SCHEDULES

Z

NOVEMBER 28, 2005

VISITING AMY'S WORK

What are you doing here James? Are you meeting Amy to take her out to lunch?

No...I just brought her this flier she wanted to photocopy.

That's so ROMANTIC!

NOVEMBER 29, 2005

I LOVE YOU TOO

There was something you wanted to tell Daddy. Do you remember?

um..

Soccer ball!

I was kinda hoping it might be "I love you"

NOVEMBER 29, 2005

CLEAR YOUR MIND

wind, wind, blow my troubles away.

And if that doesn't work, there's always the beer!

NOVEMBER 30, 2005

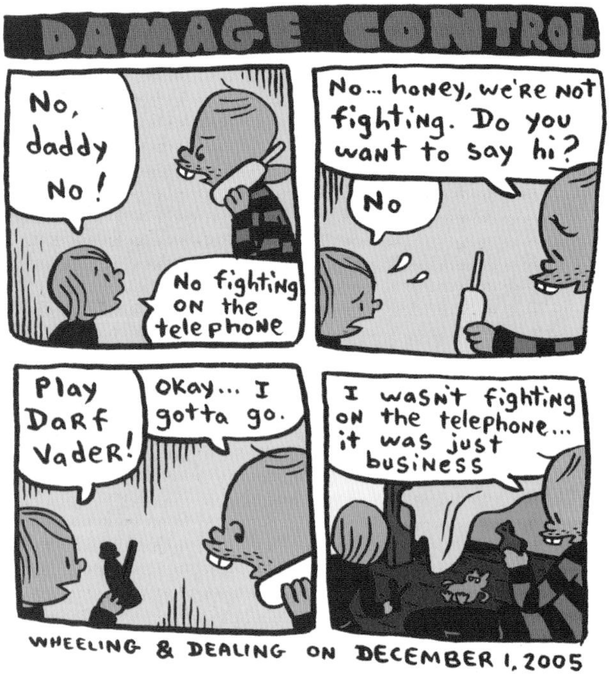
DAMAGE CONTROL
No, daddy No!
No fighting on the telephone
No... honey, we're not fighting. Do you want to say hi?
No
Play Darf Vader!
Okay... I gotta go.
I wasn't fighting on the telephone... it was just business
WHEELING & DEALING ON DECEMBER 1, 2005

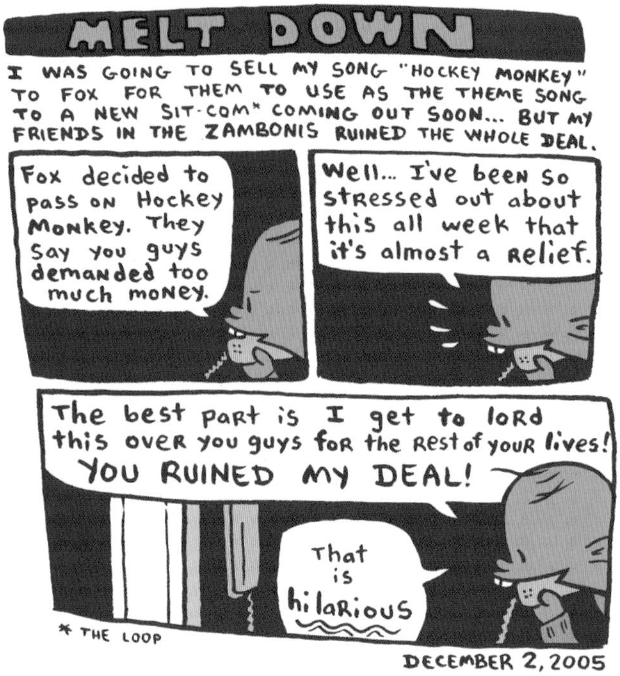
MELT DOWN
I WAS GOING TO SELL MY SONG "HOCKEY MONKEY" TO FOX FOR THEM TO USE AS THE THEME SONG TO A NEW SIT-COM* COMING OUT SOON... BUT MY FRIENDS IN THE ZAMBONIS RUINED THE WHOLE DEAL.
Fox decided to pass on Hockey Monkey. They say you guys demanded too much money.
Well... I've been so stressed out about this all week that it's almost a relief.
The best part is I get to lord this over you guys for the rest of your lives! YOU RUINED MY DEAL!
That is hilarious
* THE LOOP
DECEMBER 2, 2005

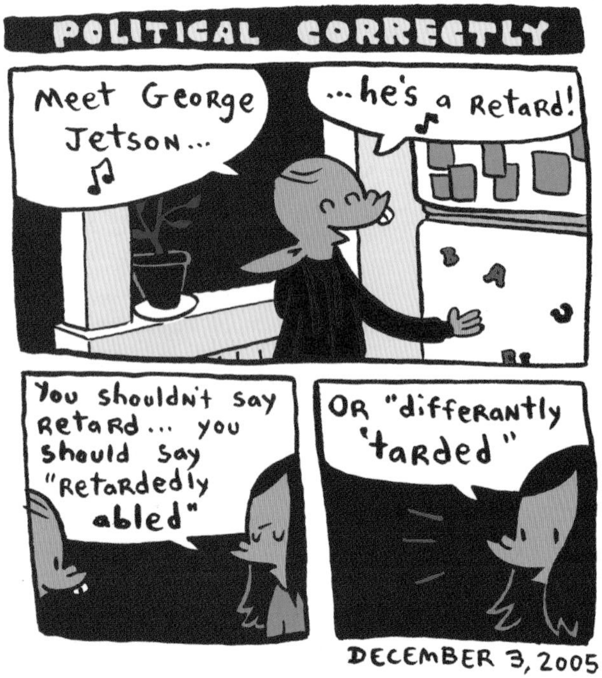
POLITICAL CORRECTLY
Meet George Jetson...
...he's a Retard!
You shouldn't say retard... you should say "retardedly abled"
Or "differantly 'tarded"
DECEMBER 3, 2005

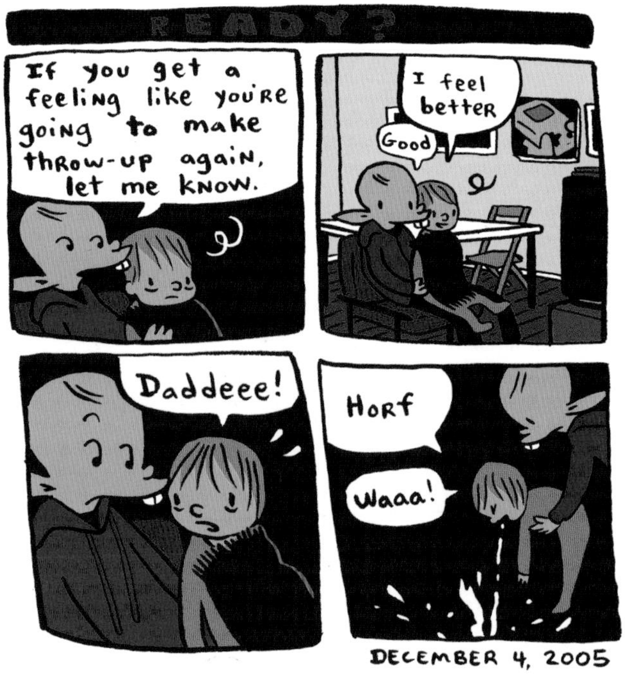
READY?
If you get a feeling like you're going to make throw-up again, let me know.
I feel better
Good
Daddeee!
Horf
Waaa!
DECEMBER 4, 2005

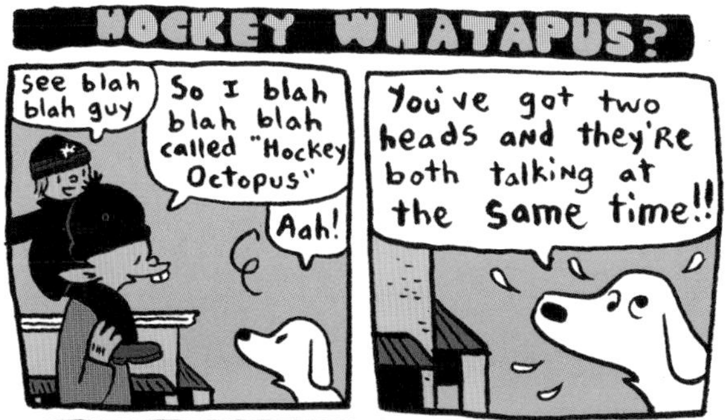
HOCKEY WHATAPUS?
See blah blah guy
So I blah blah blah called "Hockey Octopus"
Aah!
You've got two heads and they're both talking at the same time!!

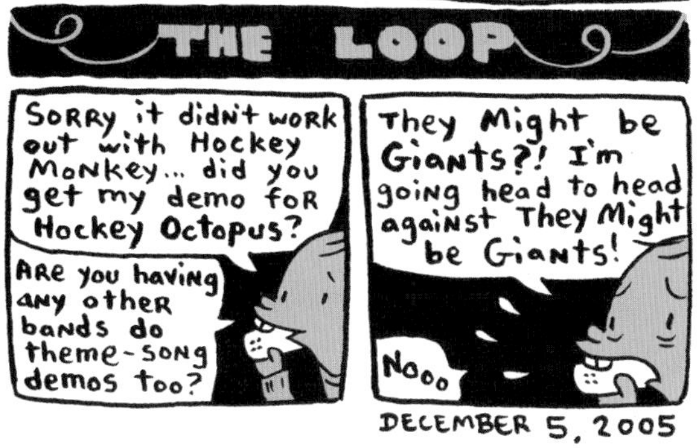
THE LOOP
Sorry it didn't work out with Hockey Monkey... did you get my demo for Hockey Octopus?
Are you having any other bands do theme-song demos too?
They Might be Giants?! I'm going head to head against They Might be Giants!
Nooo
DECEMBER 5, 2005

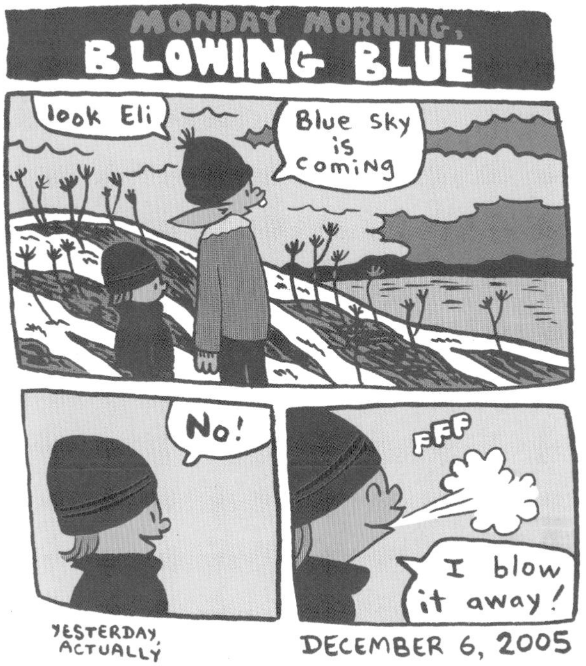
MONDAY MORNING, BLOWING BLUE
look Eli
Blue Sky is coming
No!
FFF
I blow it away!
YESTERDAY, ACTUALLY
DECEMBER 6, 2005

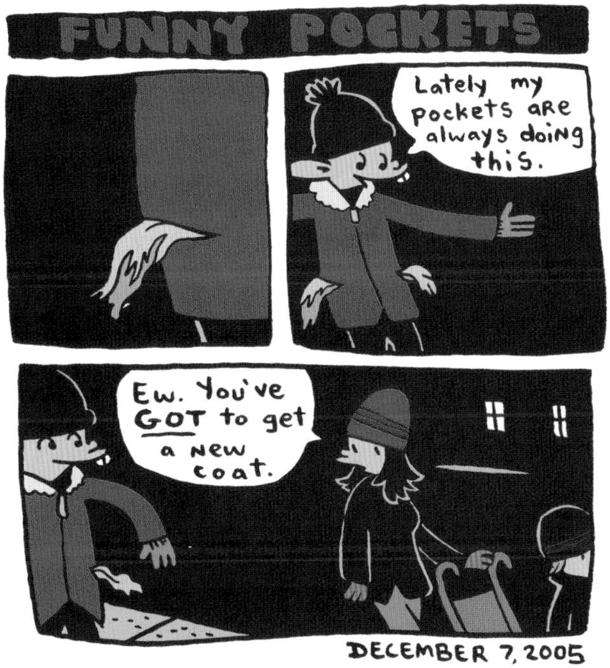
FUNNY POCKETS
Lately my pockets are always doing this.
Ew. You've GOT to get a new coat.
DECEMBER 7, 2005

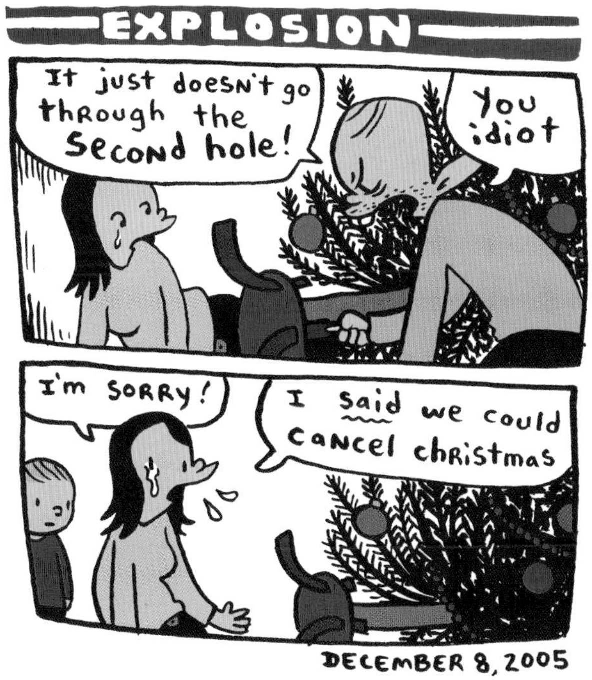
EXPLOSION
It just doesn't go through the second hole!
You idiot
I'm sorry!
I said we could cancel christmas
DECEMBER 8, 2005

RYKO SUDDENLY SOLD OFF THEIR PUBLISHING DIVISION, I NOW HAVE NO IDEA WHO ADMINISTERS MY MUSIC.

MONKEY TROUBLES

If I told people the latest twists and turns that the "Hockey Monkey" deal has taken, they'll start to think I'm a pathological liar.

When really it's just the pathological LAWYERS!

tee hee

STRESSED OUT

Yeah... I'm doing GREAT.

Well... I feel like I'm going to DIE, but besides that I'm great!

DECEMBER 9, 2005

STRESS COCOON

Don't you want to go to Josh's party?

No... I'll just stay home and take a nap. You go without me.

SOON

I can't fall asleep!

DECEMBER 10, 2005

FROM ACROSS THE GYM

They just stacked those gym mats too high.

They'll topple over

ELI!

when his head hit the floor I thought he was going to fall into a coma and die.

DECEMBER 11, 2005

BASEMENT

Let's see what that old contract says

Fuck

Fuck

The only thing that sucks about having a wife and child you adore is that suicide is no longer an option.

ha!

DECEMBER 12, 2005

SALTY SIDEWALKS

Salty Sidewalks

If I was a monster I would lick them

DECEMBER 13, 2005

A WINTER'S NAP

Eli, stay here while I go check to see if the fire is burning right

O.K.

Ow

I burned my thumb

Let me see!

DECEMBER 14, 2005

CHOCOLATE GHOST

Have you been a good boy today?

YES!

Here's a chocolate cookie.

CHOCOLATER

Woooooooooo ooooooo

Eek! A chocolate GHOST!

Ooooh

DECEMBER 15, 2005

NATIVITY SCENE

Baby Jesus covered in snow... Daddy wipe his face.

??!

YESTERDAY:

His cheeks are pink!

DECEMBER 16, 2005

THE HOLY TRINITY

GOD
THE CREATOR
OF ALL THINGS

SANTA
REWARDS
THE GOOD

SATAN
PUNISHES
THE EVIL

DECEMBER 17, 2005

DRIVING TO KING KONG

I wish I could Remember the name of it... it was about a guy who thinks he's a genius—

—James Kochalka?

... I know it's not very "cool" to go around thinking you're a genius...

But I just can't shake the feeling.

DECEMBER 18, 2005

MOTION DETECTOR LIGHTS

I was waking up all night worrying about how those lights wouldn't turn off.

I even had dreams about it

Don't worry, I fixed it.

What did you do?

Nothing. But I think it's fixed

I don't think that's what I was REALLY worried about anyway.

DECEMBER 19, 2005

BLARG!

You got a haircut today!

So handsome!

I also let my lawyers send a "cease and desist" letter to the guys who are ripping off Monkey vs. Robot

That will be a nice Christmas present for them, right?

heh heh

≥sigh≤

DECEMBER 20, 2005

TAPE A NAP

You're not sleepy at all?

No!

Well, let's go wrap your present for Mommy then.

O.K.

I help

Yes

You're helping

ZHUK

here, daddy

Tape!

Um

DECEMBER 21, 2005

STAGE MOVES

The fairy leap

Michael Jackson knee

Demonic possession

DECEMBER 22, 2005

SHE WANTS SOMETHING

Meow

Amy... Spandy says she wants an X-box 360 for Christmas!

Nmm.

BRUSH BRUSH

DECEMBER 23, 2005

WARM SNOW

INDOOR / OUTDOOR THERMOMETER

Oh! It's getting warm. That means the snow will be getting very sticky.

Eli! We're gonna make a SNOWMAN!

DECEMBER 24, 2005

WHAT I GOT

WINTER GLOVES

THE SUMMER BOOK by Tove Jansson

B.J. & DA DOGS by Ben Jones

A NEW CORDUROY JACKET

WARIOWARE TWISTED for GameBoy Advance

CHRISTMAS DECEMBER 25 2005

3 PAIRS OF EDDIE BAUER SOCKS

POORLY RESTED

Guess what! I found the "Noupa".

Oh good.

Oh good. I dreamt I was wandering homeless for decades from looking for that toy

MORNING IN NEW HAMPSHIRE, WITH AMY'S FAMILY   DECEMBER 26, 2005

MERRY PERCENTAGE

Will I ever have a 100% MERRY Christmas?

SCRATCH ITCH

Ho ho ho! Mooody Christmas, everyone!

DECEMBER 27, 2005

RE-GIFTING PARTY

Can I play with your boobies?

After the party

maybe

AFTER THE PARTY

GAK

boobies

DECEMBER 28, 2005

THOSE CROWS

An egg sandwich fell out of the sky!

DARTH VADER VS. THE MONSTERS

It's the monsters' mommy on the phone.

She says stop chasing them! It's their bedtime and you're making them too EXCITED!

Oh!

DECEMBER 29, 2005

WHAT?

So... what ARE you doing at Colin's tonight? Is it a SECRET? You've been acting weird about it all week.

Secret?? There's no secret! Ha ha ha!

LATER

Hey... can you keep a secret?

DECEMBER 30, 2005

THE... TWO DAYS

Should I give Amy her surprises today or tomorrow?

But I CAN'T wait!

Tomorrow is the 20th anniversary of our first kiss...

...but today was the day that I knew that I WANTED to kiss her...

DECEMBER 31, 2005

KOCHALKA FAMILY PHOTOGRAPHS
200... 2005

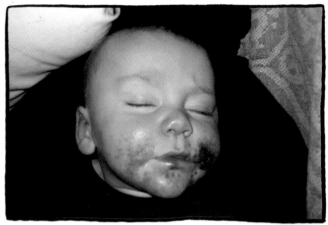

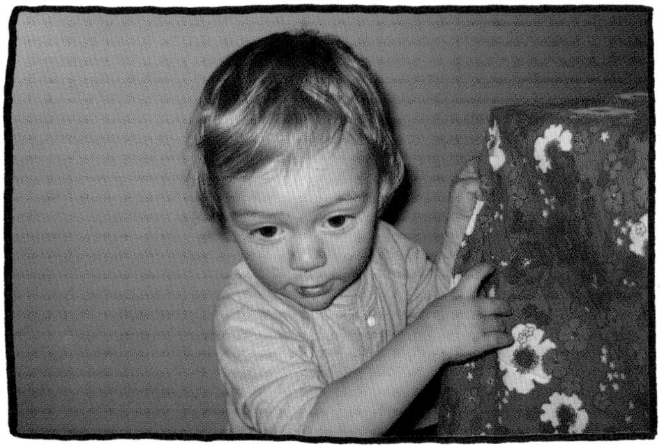

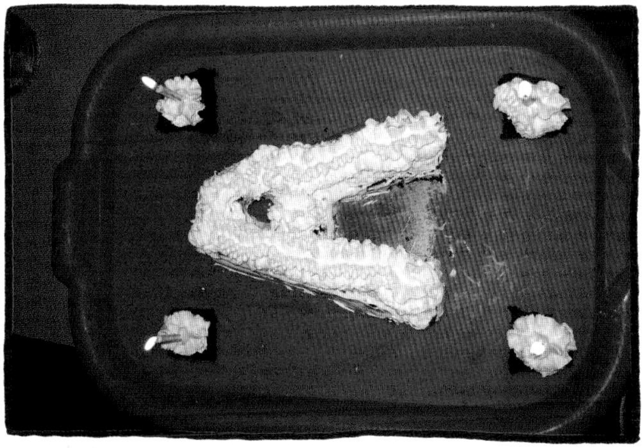

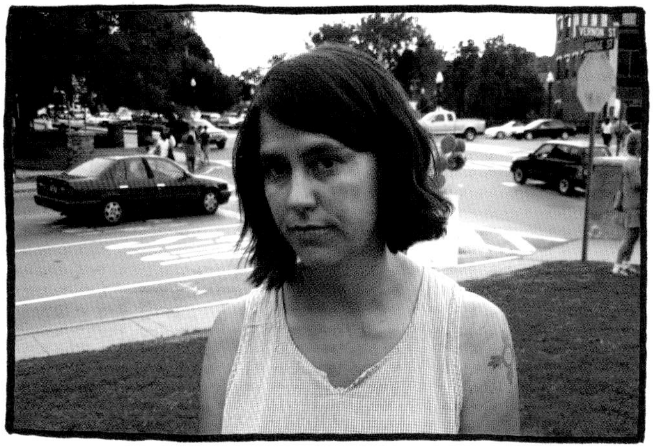
VERNON ST

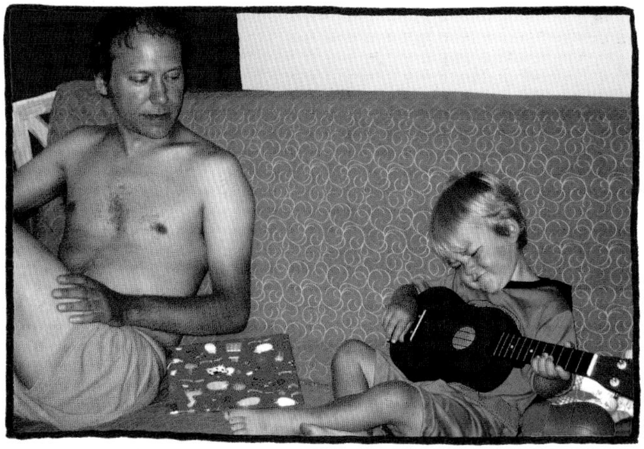

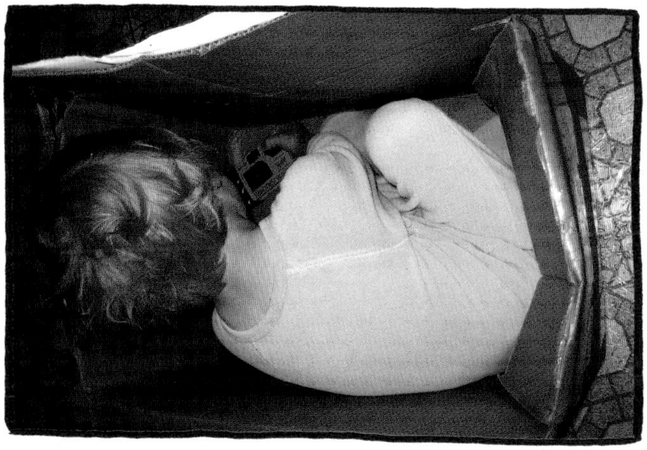

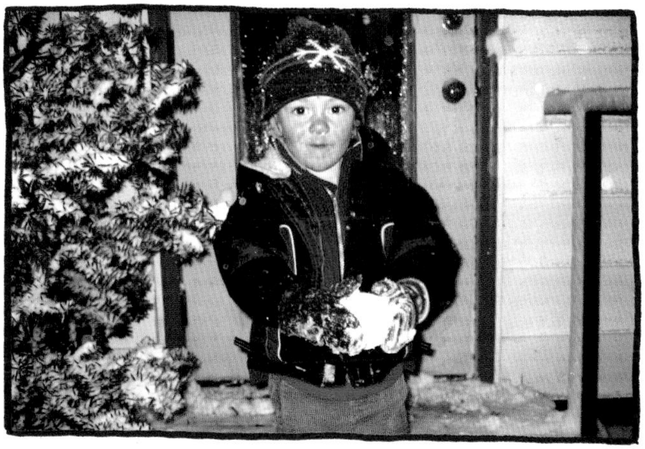